I have observed Johnny Hunt and
And I have used various words to ɑ
integrity, visionary, servant, characteᵣ
I have yearned to do is to sit down with ᵦᵢₗ Hᵤₙₜ ₐₙd let him share
with me his philosophy of leadership. I knew that such a moment
would be some of the best training I could receive. I no longer have
to wait. Johnny Hunt has written the book that tells this story.
I hope to get *Building Your Leadership Résumé* into as many hands
as possible. But first I must learn from this dear servant as I hear
from my good friend and the great God he serves.

—Thom S. Rainer
President and CEO
LifeWay Christian Resources

Johnny Hunt clearly demonstrates how God is the ultimate
model of a leader: faithfully at work in our lives for our good and
in ways that we often cannot even imagine. I have gained much
from Johnny over the years, both in his teaching and example, and
I trust the reader will be richly rewarded as well. This is a much-
needed book for our time.

—Ravi Zacharias, author and speaker

Johnny Hunt knows and loves God's leaders. And God's leaders know and love Johnny Hunt! He has proven to be one of the
most passionate and compassionate leaders of our day. His life is
a prototype for all of us to emulate. His example is a challenging
profile in what a leader should be. These pages will prove to be a
map to successful leadership and ministry in every life. It is a must
read for those whom God has called to be His ministry leaders!

—Jimmy Draper
President Emeritus, LifeWay Christian Resources

BUILDING *Your* LEADERSHIP RÉSUMÉ

Developing *the* Legacy That Will Outlast You

JOHNNY M. HUNT

B&H
PUBLISHING GROUP
NASHVILLE, TENNESSEE

ISBN: 978-0-8054-4964-8

Published by B&H Publishing Group
Nashville, Tennessee

Dewey Decimal Classification: 303.3
Subject Heading: LEADERSHIP / CHRISTIAN
LIFE / WISDOM

4 5 6 7 8 9 10 • 18 17 16 15 14

Dedicated to Janet Allen Hunt.

For the last thirty-eight years, I have been privileged to call Janet my wife. No single individual has ever cared more about me or loved me more deeply and unconditionally than this beautiful, dear lady. She has known me at my best and seen me at my worst, yet no one has been a greater encouragement for me to seek the Lord, to desire His best, and attempt to accomplish in my life that for which Christ placed me here.

Janet, thank you, thank you, thank you! You are more than any individual could imagine of what is needed in a wife that will stand by your side. You are that and more!
I deeply love you!

Acknowledgments

I would be remiss to not say thank you to the First Baptist Church Woodstock family. It is here, for the last twenty-three years, that I have had the opportunity to implement and attempt to emulate these principles. The Lord has given me a fellowship of people that have embraced God's heart and my leadership, to my great delight and joy! It has been a wonderful journey thus far to see how God has chosen to bless His dear people. In my heart, they are the greatest body of believers that exist in a local fellowship on the planet.

First Woodstock family, Miss Janet and Pastor Johnny deeply, deeply love you all! Thank you for allowing me to take the principles of God's Word, apply them in the context of the local church, and enjoy the benefits of how He always honors His promises and principles. You are the best!

—Johnny Hunt

Contents

Foreword

I have spent a lifetime studying leadership and have found two ways to unearth leadership gems. One is to research principles of leadership and then see how that principle can be applied in the real world of leading people. The second is to observe the practices and disciplines of leaders who are effectively leading . . . a leader like Johnny Hunt.

Johnny's journey of leading has spanned over the past thirty-five years since he came to know Christ personally in 1973. He has pastored four churches during that time. Every church he went to pastor was struggling upon his arrival. Every one was vibrant and alive when he left. First Baptist Church Woodstock, where he presently serves, has experienced unprecedented growth during the twenty-two years he has served there. Attendance has grown from three hundred in 1986 with an annual budget of $175,000 to an attendance today of seven thousand with an annual budget of $18,500,000. Johnny has developed many, many leaders during his years there that are serving not only at First Baptist Church Woodstock, but literally around the world.

I encourage you to read this book and then share it with your team. It will help you, instruct you, encourage you, and bless you. I am confident that if you implement these principles, you and your team will become more effective leaders.

—Dr. John Maxwell
Founder, INJOY Stewardship Services and EQUIP

Introduction

When I was in my late teens, I spent most of my time in the pool halls of Wilmington, North Carolina—including the time when I should have been in school. With that kind of practice availability, I got pretty good at shooting pool, enough that I used to dream of perhaps making it my living as a man. I often thought, *What an incredible life that would be, getting to do every day what I love doing . . . and getting paid to do it!*

I am so grateful to God that I get to do that—not working the billiard table, of course, but serving at the table of my Lord and Savior Jesus Christ. And loving it. And, hey, even getting paid for it! There's nothing else I'd rather be doing. There's nothing like living your calling, and nothing that satisfies a leader as much as leading.

I don't know what has brought you here. Perhaps you're already an established, effective leader, just doing what you've always done—seeking ways to continually grow and learn, opening yourself to new ideas and forgotten reminders. Perhaps you're an aspiring leader, hungry to add to your

1

bank of skills as you prepare for your moment of opportunity. Perhaps you're a struggling leader, about two pushes away from falling totally off the cliff of disillusionment. You're utterly discouraged right now, but you're giving it one last chance to see if you can somehow relocate your lost energy and inspiration.

Oh, how I hope and pray that the collected advice and experiences you're about to read will be helpful to you in whatever set of circumstances you find yourself. My desire is that you will be—as I have been in organizing and writing these chapters—inspired afresh with a deeper sense of God's hand on your life and His direction for your leadership. This book is a call to commitment, a call to consistency, and a call to intentional excellence in everything we do.

I remember a *Peanuts* comic strip that showed Charlie Brown's baseball coach addressing his hapless team. He said, "I have our statistics for the year. In each of our twelve games we almost scored a run. In nine of the games our opponents almost didn't score a run before the first out. Lucy almost caught three fly balls in right field, and one time we almost made the right play." Charlie Brown's insightful conclusion has been something I've never forgotten. He turned his face to the comic reader and said, "We led the league in almosts."

When my life is over and my legacy written, I don't want to be someone who was *almost* what God had called him to be. And I know you share that same resolve—to be used for great purposes, to effect lasting change, to have an impact on future generations so that your influence doesn't dry up and blow away at your death. Therefore, we must not be satisfied with where we've been or predisposed to limit what

God can still do through us as we grow older. He is a living God, and His calling and vision continue to live through us, changing people in the process—in ways we may not have yet dreamed.

Ron Dunn once told me that we leaders can tend to script what we want in life, then pray as if we're wanting God to sign off on our request. It's not that our requests are all bad or self-serving, but they may not yet be the desires of God for our lives, His reason for having us here. With this in mind, Ron challenged me to do what I'm challenging you to attempt as well: take a blank sheet of paper, sign your name on the bottom, and let God fill in the blanks. I can honestly say that after more than thirty years of leadership, God has done far more than I would have ever requested of Him or felt that He had in mind for me. It will be the same for you, as well, because God's will for your life is indeed God's best for your life.

Submit yourself to the Leader of all leaders. You were not only made *by* Him; you were also made *for* Him. Whatever potential remains for you as a leader—and I believe it is great—it can only be known through living out His desires for you.

So read on. And lead on. And to God be the glory.

—Johnny Hunt
Woodstock, Georgia
2009

People Are
Underchallenged

1

*The New Frontier of which I speak is not a set of promises—it
is a set of challenges. It sums up not what I intend to offer the
American people, but what I intend to ask of them.*

—JOHN F. KENNEDY

This may sound backward from conventional thinking, but I can assure you it's true: most church leaders do not expect enough of their people.

Are we guilty of overworking some? Probably so. And we should be serious about fixing that. But are many, many more of them going underutilized? Are they suffering spiritually from not being engaged in active areas of service and ministry? The answer is absolutely yes.

If you want a church filled with enthused, motivated, and productive members, don't dumb down your expectations

5

of them. Don't lower the standard. Don't follow in the leadership mold of most church leaders, who allow their people just to sit there and leave and remain underchallenged.

I believe the unspoken heart's cry of every born-again believer who is genuinely walking with God is this: to be more *like* Him and to be more *for* Him than they ever thought they could be. And yet churches have largely become places where the average member, like an engine throttled down with governors, is confined to running at comfortable, contained, and managed speeds. No one typically asks or expects any more of them.

Great leaders are those who will not accept complacency or mediocrity from indifferent people—those who are lying dormant, selling themselves short, squandering their ability to be more than they thought they could be. What they need from their leaders is the encouragement and opportunity to make tracks in the lane of ministry God has given them, going and blowing full throttle.

So why don't we lead like this?

One reason, quite honestly, is that leaders don't always have a clear vision for the church and its people—perhaps not even a vision for themselves. We cannot challenge others to embrace a mission we don't personally possess and embody. People under the lordship of Christ will always be our greatest resource for accomplishing God's kingdom priorities and activities. But we will be hesitant to ask and unsure what to expect of them if we don't know where God wants us to go.

A second, even worse reason for asking little of others is the leader's self-centeredness. When we get too entangled with our own ego, we cannot see the value in others. We become afraid to empower them. Maybe we don't think anyone can do it as good as we can—can't do it to suit us. Or maybe (if we're being honest) we just don't want to share the spotlight with anyone. Their involvement, though perhaps culminating in a better result, might dim our recognition and steal some of our glory. No leader wants to admit this, but if it's true, it's limiting your effectiveness.

As God speaks into our lives, as we receive vision from Him, and as we share that vision with our people, they will receive it, will accept the challenge, and will be changed forever. Don't expect any less!

There are people in our congregations who love Christ and want to do great things for Him. Great things! Yet all we ever ask them to do is pass an offering plate or hand out bulletins. I'm not making light of any of these functions. They are important and contribute to our service to God and to others. But people are underchallenged. They have a passion in their hearts to do more, to be more, to be an active part of something purposeful and significant. As leaders, it is our responsibility to inspire and excite them about the possibilities that exist. When we do this, many will step up and accept the challenge faithfully.

At one time our church was conducting three morning services: 8:00, 9:30, and 11:00. As we began thinking about and planning the logistics for that earliest service, we realized that pulling off the music was going to be a challenge. In order for the music team to be ready for an 8:00 service, it would mean being there ready to rehearse by 7:00—not everybody's favorite time to be awake, much less singing in your church clothes on a Sunday morning, especially when you're expected to do it again twice more before afternoon.

But what if we could capture a vision for the early service and create an opportunity for others to take leadership in our music ministry? What if we could show them the key role they could play in our church's life, worship, and witness?

Enter the student choir and orchestra. Eager for the chance to sing and play on a regular basis for the entire church body, they excitedly took on the challenge. We were asking a lot. Sunday at 7:00 a.m. is even earlier for teenagers and young adults. This was going to require a real commitment of time and reliability. But as a result, not only was the music in our early service provided capably and with spiritual energy, our student program grew and improved with the added responsibility given to them.

Church leaders must empower the entrusted if our people are ever to reach their God-given potential, both personally and corporately. We must help them see the benefits that naturally occur when leadership and participation become everyone's responsibility. That's why the wisest leaders recognize the needs and motivations of their fellow servants, and consider this an essential component of one's leadership résumé. Understanding other people's abilities and dreams enables the leader to develop more leaders, producing a richer, more vibrant, and more satisfied and effective ministry team.

The voices of complacency and sameness say, "If you ask more of people, expect to get pushed back." The truth is, challenging people to greater things will lead to the best days you've ever known.

Everyone desires to be on a winning team. It's our responsibility as leaders to help them see that what they're doing is significant and making a difference—a big difference—both in *their* lives and in others, as well as for God's glory.

So raise the bar. Set the standard high. Let people realize how important their work is. Stop underchallenging them from fear that they'll revolt and tell you no. Start expecting more, and watch what God will do in their lives.

A Leader's Passion

2

We may affirm absolutely that nothing great in the world has been accomplished without passion.

—GEORG WILHELM FRIEDRICH HEGEL

A lmost nothing can stop passion.

You can have all the talent, ability, and spiritual giftedness in the world. You can be a diesel engine with high capacity and tons of horsepower. But that big train will take you only so far unless there's fuel in the tank. And the fuel in the tank of leadership is high-octane, premium-strength passion.

Nothing better can get in the way of that.

Passionate leaders develop a "whatever it takes" mentality. They know their life's calling. They know the purpose and direction God has given them. They know the ministry tasks that lie before them. But most of all, they know how to turn that knowledge into action. They're willing to face the inevitable challenges of leadership with drive, guts, and get-after-it persistence.

Passion sees no unstoppable barriers. It will plow through, jump across, or dig under any obstacles. Where some see a dead end, passion sees a possibility. Where some grow tired from the struggle, passion is energized to see it through. Where some are ready to quit, passion rocks on. Passion is only getting started when others are conceding failure.

People often ask me, "Where do you get your energy? How do you stay motivated?" I believe part of the answer is what artist and sculptor Henry Moore found: "The secret of life is to have a task, something you devote your entire life to, something you bring everything to, every minute of the day for the rest of your life." But what keeps me going in particular—and what can keep you going as well—is a passion for Christ and His Word, passion for His people, and passion for the calling He's placed upon your life.

Passion for God. This is indeed the first and greatest of all commandments—to "love the Lord your God with all your heart, with all your soul, with all your strength, and with all your mind" (Luke 10:27). The apostle Paul put it this way, "For me, living is Christ" (Phil. 1:21). That was his number-one passion. For him, Jesus' name was a word synonymous with "living." Like food to the belly, passion for Christ is fuel and energy to the human spirit, not just for pastors but for all believers. Leadership begins with a passion for God.

Passion for others. Jesus tabbed this as the second greatest commandment—to love "your neighbor as yourself"

(Luke 10:27). When Paul said his final farewells to the Ephesian church leaders, he assured them that he had not shrunk back from proclaiming anything to them that was profitable, "or from teaching it to you in public and from house to house" (Acts 20:20). To the Corinthians he promised, "I am not seeking what is yours, but you. . . . I will most gladly spend and be spent for you" (2 Cor. 12:14–15). Giving to others and investing in others should always be part of a leader's passion and résumé.

Passion for ministry. When a leader has passion, he sells out for the cause. He goes all in. He has a fire in his bones, a zeal that can hardly be contained, knowing that God has called him to this work. Therefore no action or effort is too much to expend. Paul said, "If I preach the gospel, I have no reason to boast, because an obligation is placed on me." In fact, "Woe to me if I do not preach the gospel!" (1 Cor. 9:16). Passion eliminates certain words from our vocabulary—words like *retreat, compromise, surrender, halfheartedness.* Passion knows the joy of immersing oneself in a worthy endeavor until no other way of living—or leading—will do. Passion works. Passion perseveres. Passion fires the soul, causing impossibilities to vanish.

But if it's not there, how do you get it? If you don't feel it, how do you possess it?

1. *Realize that God desires passionate people.* "He gave Himself for us to redeem us from all lawlessness and to cleanse for Himself a special people, eager to do good works" (Titus 2:14)—zealous to be about His business. Paul reminds us not to "lack diligence; be fervent in spirit; serve the Lord" (Rom. 12:11). If you want what God wants, then you want to be a passionate leader.

2. *Pray for passion.* I heard of a Mississippi country preacher who mounted the pulpit one morning and prayed, "Lord, give thy servant this day the eyes of the eagle and the wisdom of the owl. Illuminate my brow with the sun of heaven. Possess my mind with love for the people. Turpentine my imagination, grease my lips, electrify my brain with the lightning of the Word. Fill me plumb full of the dynamite of thy glory. Anoint me all over with the kerosene of salvation, and set me on fire. Amen." Now there's a man who knew what passion is—and knew that it only comes from the Lord. Pray for passion.

3. *Believe that passion is the deciding difference in your life.* Nineteenth-century philosopher Søren Kierkegaard warned of danger if the church ever lost her passion for the gospel, if she treated it instead like a piece of information. When true passion is substituted by mere descriptions of passion, Kierkegaard compared it to reading a cookbook to a starving man. Passion cannot be replaced. It is an elemental essential.

4. *Know that passion has more influence than personality.* Everyone has a personality, but not everyone possesses passion. Your personality may or may not inspire. It may change depending on circumstances. It may be one thing today and another thing tomorrow. But passion can be constant—and can be constantly having an impact. Paul told how the zeal of the Corinthians had "stirred up" other churches to give generously to support the believers in Jerusalem (2 Cor. 9:2). Don't depend on your personality to make a difference. Passion takes over where natural charisma leaves off.

5. *Return to your first love.* You'll experience a passion leak if you let anything but Christ wake you up in the

morning. If you ever lower your focus to let outward success be your motivator—or people's opinions, or financial growth, or your upcoming vacation—the needle will start to dip on your passion meter. That's because only Christ can continually supply and never run out. As He warned the church in Ephesus, don't abandon "the love you had at first" (Rev. 2:4). Don't grow misguided or apathetic. Apathy is not a state of mind but a state of the heart. And it will steal what's left of your passion. Don't let it.

6. *Associate with people of passion.* Just as one log cannot burn by itself, neither can one passionate person afford to go it alone. Surround yourself with other burning logs, and they will keep yours from burning out.

Passion will separate you from the crowd. It will give you unquenchable desire, an all-consuming drive. If you've noticed an energy drop in your zeal for leadership, passion will restore excitement and extravagance to your ministry. Like Mary, who took the expensive perfume and poured it on the feet of the Lord Jesus, your passion for Him and the work He's given you will turn heads in the room.

Be bold. Be strong. Be passionate.

Focus

3

Concentrate your energies, your thoughts, and your capital. The wise man puts all his eggs in one basket and watches the basket.

—ANDREW CARNEGIE

A whole lot of your worst distractions can come disguised as good ideas. They're things you want to do, things you believe you'd be good at, things that tempt your "whatever it takes" mentality. But sometimes, what you need is to take a step back to see if this new opportunity fits within your life's calling and cause.

What it takes at times like these is *focus*.

Churches, for example, can quickly become clearing houses for all kinds of ministries and activities. And while these look real nice on a Web site, if a substantial number of them are outside the scope of your church's focus, you could be leading your congregation into a whirlwind of flurry and motion with little or no forward progress.

Lots of churches today have plenty of speed, but they don't seem to know which direction they're going. They've saddled themselves to too many horses—sometimes to horses that died a long time ago! As a leader, you must know when it's time to unsaddle the horse so you can move on (or move back) to those vehicles that have the best chance of carrying your vision forward.

Through the years I've noticed several key principles that can help leaders stay anchored to their core priorities, to stay focused. See if these apply to you:

1. *Pursue excellence one thing at a time.* Better to be your absolute best at a single pursuit than to be mediocre at a whole bunch of them. As an example, our church at Woodstock believes the main thing that reaches the most people is our Sunday morning worship. Therefore, those of us with leadership responsibilities in that area put our best energy and focus into making this hour everything God wants it to be. We even refer to it as Super Bowl Sunday— every week. It's a big deal to us! The atmosphere needs to be just right for people to hear from God. The music and preaching must be well prepared and fervently prayed over. Company's coming, and lives are at stake. So like a football team amping up to be their best on game day, we make every Sunday morning our focus all week long.

As a result of pouring everything into one thing, you'll find (as we have) that God will bring new leaders on board who can bring *their* focus to the other elements of ministry: Sunday night, Wednesday night, small groups, and all the other outreaches that issue forth from your congregation.

But don't try to do it all at once. Do your main thing well—with excellence—and God will supply you with people and resources to do more.

2. *Be who you are.* Churches today are all over the map in terms of strategy and methodology. If we're not careful, we'll try to determine our own church's focus by looking at others and seeing how they're doing it. Listen, the reason God didn't *make* us all the same is because He doesn't want all of us to *be* the same. Certainly we do share some basic biblical purposes that are the same across the board, but your church has an identity and focus that others do not. So before you run wild copying ministry strategies that are working in other places, find out who you are; then build your strategies to carry out your church's vision.

One of the quickest ways to wear people out is to keep them jumping from one plan and program to the next, never quite accomplishing one before cranking up another. Sooner or later you must settle on the methods and ministries that match your church's focus, then stick to them while God works in your midst to achieve His goals. If you chase two rabbits, both of them will get away from you.

3. *Focused churches start with focused leaders.* An interviewer once asked pianist Victor Borge if he played any other instruments. "Yes," he replied, "my other piano." You yourself can't be strong in all facets of ability and personality. You can't play every instrument. You can't do everything. A focused leader knows this and puts people around himself who can fill in where he is lacking, delegating to others who can do what he cannot.

You have many gifts that make you who you are. It's up to you to keep them focused, to keep them active, to keep them sharp. Don't dull what you do well by laboring at what you do poorly. Let others embrace your vision, then they can bring their own energy and talents to bear on your shared ministry.

4. *Manage yourself well.* Focused leaders put great emphasis on managing the following: their time, priorities, resources, budget, people, and influence. Successful ministries—those that are truly effective for the kingdom of God—don't just happen on their own. Neither do successful lives. They are always the result of planning, sacrifice, and focus. Bob Buford, in his landmark book *Half Time*, wrote, "I'm convinced that many people never make it to a life of significance because they're trapped in a lifestyle that won't let them." My, how true that is! Some leaders will never manage to become useful and fruitful because they're unwilling to manage themselves.

Some churches are the same way. I'm convinced the reason we have so many small churches today is because they're *designed* to be small. They're organized that way. They're comfortable that way. They're led that way. And until they change to a model of growth and real vision, they'll never reach beyond where they already are. Strive to be a better steward of what God has given you to shepherd and oversee.

5. *Do a little weedeating.* Not everything that grows in a garden is good. Occasionally we need to clear away some of the unwanted or underperforming parts so the healthy growth has room to prosper and thrive. As I said, churches can often be the worst at getting overextended into all kinds of efforts and initiatives. These ideas seem to make perfect sense when we plant them—and usually they do serve a

valid purpose for a time—but after a while they can lose their focus. Soon they're sapping resources that could be better used somewhere else, or they're going to seed from lack of careful attention.

Focus your church's energies on what you do well. Accentuate the few things that produce the most fruit. Spend time on things that really matter, things that really make a difference. And everyone around you will *see* the difference.

I dare say that people have never had more demands on their personal time than they do today. Therefore, churches cannot be in the business of squandering their members' schedules by expecting them to be part of things that don't function well or don't meet legitimate needs. If we're going to make a difference with the short time we have left in this world, both we and our churches must remain focused.

It's been said that we'll have all eternity to enjoy our victories but only one life in which to win them. Focus is what keeps our "one life" trained on the things God has called us to do.

Empowering the Entrusted

4

Trust a man in nothing who has not a conscience in everything.

—Laurence Sterne

I believe in believing in people. I hope you do too. But in order to be an effective leader, this warm, welcoming attitude must be counterbalanced by another: you must avoid delegating responsibility to the irresponsible. Don't entrust those who cannot be trusted.

Most new leaders, whether they head up a church or some other kind of organization, are concerned about surrounding themselves with people who can share the load. These selected men and women are tasked with carrying large portions of responsibility, becoming like the leader's right or left arm. They must be able to function without needing their hands held. They must be capable of taking ownership over their selected areas of emphasis. They must be people with drive, determination, and good decision-making skills. They are your leadership team, and you will be counting on them heavily as you steer this enterprise in the direction you envision.

Perhaps you already know from experience—or will trust those of us who've been there—that few things are more frustrating in leadership than dealing with the fact that you've picked the wrong person to help you.

Sometimes we choose too quickly. Sometimes we don't know enough about this individual. Sometimes we simply misread their character or put too much trust in listings on a résumé. But digging out from under this mistake is no fun at all—not only for you but also for them. So when it comes to building your team, be very careful that you only empower those who are worthy of your trust. If you don't, you will definitely pay for it later. As some have said, giftedness can carry some people to places their character cannot sustain them.

OK—with that point made, let's steer away from the negative and look at this in a more positive light. For not only is it true that some people shouldn't be entrusted with positions of leadership, it's also true that those who *can* be entrusted . . . *should.* Unlike the character in Shakespeare's *As You Like It* who said, "Love all, trust a few," a leader can't afford to be quite so guarded and extreme. In order to lead, you may have to put your trust in *many* people. But you do need to be sure that you are seeing them with your eyes wide open.

Let some of these key attitudes guide your thinking:

1. *It really does begin with believing in people.* Paul believed in Timothy. Elijah believed in Elisha. Moses believed in

Joshua. Jesus believed in Simon Peter—enough that He changed the disciple's name from "wavering one" to "the rock." Now this wasn't because Peter had shown a tremendous track record up to that point. But Jesus had been watching. *Really* watching! And instead of seeing only who Peter *was*, He could also see what Peter had the potential of becoming. For this reason He trusted Peter with a great work, even though He knew this bullheaded fisherman would still make many mistakes along the way to becoming the leader Jesus saw in him. Seeing the potential—believing in people—is a big part of successful leadership.

Jesus acted on His belief in Peter's potential on numerous occasions. You'll remember that He called Peter to walk on the water to Him. In doing so, He was giving Peter the opportunity to fail, but He was also teaching him visually— unforgettably—the importance of keeping His eyes on Christ at all times. The Bible reveals scenes when Jesus both blessed and corrected Peter—sometimes harshly—but in each case He was preparing him for greater things in the future. Jesus believed in this man. He could see something in Peter that He knew would eventually blossom into fruitfulness. So He spoke words of challenge. He spoke words of encouragement. And all of it spoke volumes to this budding leader's heart. Don't be afraid to believe in people. Actively seek them out. Look for those who give you the impression that God is up to something special in their lives.

2. *Support people.* If you're going to entrust someone with a certain task or responsibility, know that this entrusting comes with the matching responsibility of encouraging them and being there for them. Turn your hindsight into their foresight. Show them how to learn from their (and your)

mistakes, using these as springboards to future success. But don't be hypercritical, making them gun-shy or afraid to try new things. Focus 80 percent of your attention on what people do right, and 20 percent on correcting what's wrong. Be real, be honest, but be on their side. Let them know you're behind them.

Part of this means putting them in places where they can utilize their strengths, not being force-fit into a role that isn't conducive to them. We're tempted to surround ourselves with people who play to *our* strengths, who already think like we think or share our same likes and abilities. The truth is, your team already has someone like you—*you!*—and they don't really need another one. What you need now are people who complement you, who add variety, who broaden the imagination and talent base of the whole group. Don't expect everyone to be like you. That would make for a very boring church. Instead, let people use what God has built into their lives by opening up opportunities for them and supporting what they do.

3. *Invest in people.* Let them travel with you. Allow them to attend conferences and training events in their area of responsibility. Assign them preaching opportunities, perhaps a wedding or a funeral. Ask them to research something for you. Enlist them to be part of helping you deal with a particular issue in the church. Give them the freedom to make decisions and implement their strategies. Network them with other successful leaders, enabling them to be influenced by those who have influenced you. Prove that you have confidence in them. Invest in them!

Jesus allowed His disciples to take ownership of the ministry He had created. What about you? Do you make yourself available to teach and mentor others? Is this a deliberate item on your schedule? Those who develop into effective leaders always point back to someone—a pastor, a teacher, a coach—who helped them along life's journey. Will others refer to you as someone who really poured yourself into them, equipping them for the challenges their future would hold? Successful leaders share their knowledge and experience with others.

4. *Challenge people*. We're in the people business. The greatest resource the body of Christ has are people. And one of our main jobs as leaders is to call forth energy and enthusiasm from them, inspiring them to reach beyond their potential, to help them see what happens when their availability meets God's empowerment.

Jesus once asked His disciples, "Who do people say that the Son of Man is?" (Matt. 16:13). Then He seemed to personalize the question to Peter: "But you, . . . who do you say that I am?" (Matt. 16:15). When Peter answered with his declaration of Christ's divinity, Jesus affirmed him by saying, "Simon son of Jonah, you are blessed because flesh and blood did not reveal this to you, but My Father in heaven" (Matt. 16:17). Peter had been challenged, and God had supercharged him with faith and boldness.

Any person worth his or her salt wants a good challenge, especially when its fulfillment will deepen their relationship with Christ and confirm their usefulness in the work of the kingdom. So don't hold back from believing in them, supporting them, and investing in them—empowering the entrusted to fulfill their unique contributions to the team.

The Dos and Don'ts of Empowerment

5

*A professor can never better distinguish himself in his work
than by encouraging a clever pupil.*

—CARL LINNAEUS

This business of "empowering people" may sound like
the work of stirring speeches and pep talks. But I can
assure you, it is much more practical than that. Getting
people fired up for the work God has already called and
equipped them to accomplish is a matter of everyday dos
and don'ts on the leader's part—things like:

Don't assume too much power and control. Get it through
your mind that this church, this ministry, this organization—
whatever kind of enterprise God has called you to lead—is not
about you. It rests on the efforts, enthusiasm, and innovation
of a whole lot of people. So don't worry about making yourself

irreplaceable. Be generous in passing leadership responsibilities along to others. Delegate well and freely.

Don't enlist from the pulpit. People don't often respond to the roundup and the cattle call. The ones who do are usually the same ones who volunteer for everything else. Most people who have never served as a leader are timid to take the reins, and they require a more personal nudge. So if you've had your eyes on particular persons who have potential in a given area, set up a special meeting. Invite them to your office. Visit them at home. Take them out to eat. Share the importance of what you're asking them to do. Encourage them to pray about it for a few days, ensuring them you'll be praying about it as well. You'll be surprised what people will do when they know you need them, when they truly feel empowered to serve.

Don't operate on the theory of "my way or the highway." You'll never lead well through intimidation. Rather than achieving a cohesive team, the practice of forcing uniformity only reveals insecurity in you as a leader. Control freaks and micromanagers neither inspire nor empower. The truth is, respectful disagreement is healthy for an organization. When everyone agrees about everything, we often refer to ourselves as having unity. What we are, however, is unhealthy. Encourage open, honest opinions. It's good for you, good for everybody.

Don't demand loyalty—earn it. Building on Don't #3, the surest way to keep from getting your team's respect is to demand it. Loyalty is a two-way street. You can't have it if you don't give it out. When you're loyal to your people, they will be loyal to you in return. They'll feel empowered. They'll want to work hard for you.

Don't intervene when others can work it out for themselves. When someone brings an issue to me and asks me to solve their problem, I often tell them to pray about it. I ask them to come back later and share with me what they've discovered, what they now believe to be the best approach to handling it. Then I usually empower them to use what they've gained from this season of thinking and prayer to be part of the solution themselves. If we always solve everyone's problems, no one else develops the skills to make good decisions without our input.

Don't hoard information—share information. As a good rule of thumb, I've found it's better to share a little too much information than to withhold it. Information is vital to the decision-making process of your team. And if everything stays within a narrow, inaccessible wall of silence, others feel restricted and uninvolved, kept in their place. They can't participate with you in offering their opinions. Good people will tend to do the right thing with information. Plus, they'll sense your empowerment by your willingness to share it with them.

Don't be indecisive. Decide who should decide. In some cases *you'll* need to decide. In most cases, however, someone else should decide. So empower them to take ownership of the matter. Remember this: 95 percent of the decisions made throughout the course of the week will have little or no impact beyond the immediate moment, so concentrate your energies on the 5 percent that do have impact. Leave the other 95 percent to someone else.

Don't be afraid of mistakes. Life is full of them. So accept the fact that mistakes will take place every day. Learn from your mistakes and move on.

Don't expect everyone to produce at the same level. God didn't make us with the same abilities nor with the same capacity for executing them. Everyone is different. The main issue is making sure everyone is empowered to make the most of what they do have.

But just as there are many things to avoid when it comes to empowerment, the leader has a lot of ways to positively affect what happens around him:

Do see your team as allies, not enemies. Don't view your people with suspicion and doubt. See them as an extension of your ministry, as partners with you in this great work to be done. For when they win, you win. And when both of you win, the entire team wins.

Do allow others to step forward and assume leadership roles. A child will never learn to ride a bike if he's never allowed to scuff up his pants. Give people a clear vision and let them run with it. Inspire them by your example, and empower them to go make a difference themselves.

Do encourage cooperation. Live by the philosophy that says everyone will prosper or no one will. Never leave someone behind. There will always be those who abandon ship, but don't abandon anyone by your own negligence or your failure to recognize them. Remember, we're all in this together. Each team member needs all the others.

Do lead by example. Winston Churchill said, "You cannot build a staff as you build a house, from the bottom upwards, and then when it is all finished, put the chief of staff on top of it like the chimney." As a leader, you must be active and engaged, exerting yourself with the same intensity you expect from others, driven by the same vision you're rallying the whole team around. For "if the trumpet makes an unclear sound, who will prepare for battle?" (1 Cor. 14:8). But if others see you living this vision with your own sweat and tears, they will be empowered to join you, sharpening themselves like iron against iron, each person sharpening the other (see Prov. 27:17).

Do learn to let go. Know what you want, provide guidance, but leave the details to others. Trust them enough to take your hands off the hyperdrive controls and let them engage their own ingenuity. You'll all be encouraged—perhaps even surprised—to see what God can do through each of you when you work within your calling. Maybe you didn't know you could get that kind of passion and persistence out of someone. You'll never know till you turn them loose.

Do listen to others. Sometimes we're not able to see ourselves objectively. We're so busy doing so many things, it's hard to determine with self-perceived clarity which of our leadership activities are really making a difference, which ones are assisting others in staying empowered. But by making time to listen to people who are willing to speak into our lives, we get a sense for where we're being most effective so we can stay there, so we can help to keep all of us growing. The best leaders are the best listeners.

Do know the hot button for each team member. More than just providing us an accurate reflection of what people see in us, listening helps us understand what others need in order to stay empowered. Listening helps us recognize what motivates each individual—those "hot buttons" that fire their imagination and get them excited about making plans. Plug people into their passion, and you'll see the sparks fly.

Do push decision making to the lowest level possible. Why should you be making decisions about an area that someone else is an expert on? The people who eat, breathe, and sleep a particular ministry—they need to be the ones (not you) empowered to keep things clicking in their area. Allow the minister of education to make decisions on Sunday school curriculum. Allow your property management person to decide what tables and chairs to order. Allow your director of children's ministry to decide what kinds of murals to be painted on the elementary wall. Always push it down to the lowest level, and allow them to rise to the occasion.

Do know when to back off. It's important for a leader to be physically present. But too much presence can thwart people and create a team of codependents. Theodore Roosevelt said, "The best leader is the one who has sense enough to pick good people to do what he wants done, and self-restraint enough to keep from meddling with them while they do it." Empower them; don't oppress them.

This is the essence of your work—empowering workers to perpetuate and perfect your vision. It may sound all high and mighty, but it's really just part of a day's work for a devoted leader.

A Real Leader
Is a Real Giver

6

Money is like sea water; the more you drink,
the thirstier you get.

—ROMAN PROVERB

Money has been the trap of many leaders. The making of it, the manipulating of it, the misappropriating of it—there are so many ways for financial attachments and attainments to divert you from your vision. Some of the same skills you employ in attracting people to your cause can also attract money to it. And because of the nature of its allure, money has a way of getting under a leader's skin, becoming an end that justifies most any kind of means.

The wise have always known that acquiring money for its own sake is an unwise venture. King Solomon, perhaps the wisest man of all time, wrote, "The one who loves money is never satisfied with money, and whoever loves wealth is never satisfied with income" (Eccles. 5:10).

And what the wise have known, so have the wealthy. John D. Rockefeller once said, "I have made many millions, but they have brought me no happiness," to which he later added, "The poorest man I know is the man who has nothing but money." Cornelius Vanderbilt warned that "the care of millions is too great a load; there is no pleasure in it." John Jacob Astor described himself as the most miserable man on earth.

Strangely, this is the final payoff from the pursuit of money. It always ends up weighing more than it's worth. The only way to counteract this inevitable result is by inverting our attitude, becoming someone that money can only make more generous. Leaders who last are leaders who give.

Scottish theologian William Barclay said, "If a man's wealth ministers to nothing but his own pride and enriches no one but himself, it becomes his ruination because it impoverishes his soul. But if he uses it to bring help and comfort to others, in becoming poorer he really becomes richer."

Solomon again waxed wise on the subject: "One person gives freely, yet gains more; another withholds what is right, only to become poor. A generous person will be enriched, and the one who gives a drink of water will receive water" (Prov. 11:24–25). Or as Jesus put it, in His own direct way, "It is more blessed to give than to receive" (Acts 20:35).

Truly we're never more like Jesus than when we're giving. It is one of the greatest joys of the Christian life, as well as one of the hallmarks of healthy leadership.

But it doesn't start with the act of writing a check or

slipping twenties from your wallet. Giving begins with
contentment—a word that means just the opposite of *covet-
ousness*. Instead of wanting more, contentment seeks nothing else than what a person already has. "Add not to a man's
possessions," the Greek philosopher Epicurus said, "but take
away from his desires." Before we can be genuine givers, we
must be genuinely grateful for what we've been given.

Once again, Solomon revealed the peace that sincerity of
heart can bring to matters of money, when he asked God to
"Give me neither poverty nor wealth; feed me with the food
I need. Otherwise, I might have too much and deny You,
saying, 'Who is the Lord?' or I might have nothing and steal,
profaning the name of my God" (Prov. 30:8–9).

Contentment. We can hardly expect it in others if we
don't possess it ourselves. And we cannot become joyful
givers until we have it.

Three words of advice when it comes to giving:

1. *Consciously affirm that the Lord owns everything you
have.* You and I are mere stewards of what we've been given.
It all belongs to the Lord. We *know* that, but do we *live* like
it's so? Do we let it lead logically to the question: How can
I advance the kingdom or make my ministry more effective
with the possessions God has blessed me with?

2. *Cultivate a thankful heart.* God owes us nothing.
Anything received from Him should make us grateful. It's
all about grace.

3. *Distinguish wants from needs.* How much more money
would be available for the Lord's work if each of us under-
took this one act of reanalysis—if we spent less than we
made, if we had a renewed basis for giving sacrificially to
the Lord?

Often in the context of giving, I find myself focused on the judgment seat of Christ. I think of the day when I will stand before the Lord and give an account for what I have done with my time, my talents, and my treasures. I don't believe He will call us into account for things He didn't gift us to accomplish or for resources we didn't give because we didn't have them. But as far as the bounty of gifts, talent, and time He has deposited into our lives, I do believe we'll have to give an accounting for this. He'll want to know what kind of return He received on His investment in us. We should stand in this posture more often than we do—living within view of eternity, right here on earth. It would change the way we live . . . and the way we give.

I challenge you to step up to the plate in your practice of giving. If this has not been an area where you've experienced much freedom and joy up to now, open yourself to its possibilities and discover it for yourself. Those who follow you will not respond to your words of challenge as much as they'll respond to the witness of your lifestyle. They will deem giving as important when they see you actually doing it, not just talking about it. If you want your people to be committed givers, it'll take a giving commitment on your part. No two ways about it.

In the familiar story of the Good Samaritan, Jesus introduces us to three characters (and their leading characteristics): the taker, the keeper, and the giver. The taker has the mind-set that what's yours is mine and I'm going to take it. The keeper says that what's mine is mine and I'm going to keep it. But the giver always says what's mine is yours and I'm going to give it. In any church or organization, there are always takers, keepers, and givers. I'm of the deep personal conviction that the happiest people in life are those who've decided to be givers. I pray that you will be like the giver in the story of the Good Samaritan, for it represents none other than the Lord Jesus.

Guiding
Principles

7

> *He whose heart is firm, and whose conscience approves his conduct, will pursue his principles unto death.*
>
> —THOMAS PAINE

Very few would deny the fact that leaders are held to a higher standard. But no one should hold us to a higher standard than we do ourselves. Speaking for myself as a pastor, no church on the planet could require more of me than I'm willing to give. And even then—regardless of anyone's expectation of me or of us—we should be solidly aware that the Lord Jesus is worthy of our absolute best. He deserves nothing less than excellence.

A higher standard for leaders? You bet. We shouldn't want it any other way. We do the best we can, or we do it over. It's as simple as that.

The only question that remains for the leader is what this higher standard looks like. What are the guiding principles that can keep us performing at high levels, that can keep us effective in our callings?

1. *Adopt godly values.* The way a person thinks within himself, so is he (see Prov. 23:7). If we want to be godly on the outside, we must make sure we're growing more godly on the inside every day, where nobody sees but us. God places His vision into those whose hearts are beating to the right values. Our standard should be the Scripture. Our role model should be Christ Jesus.

2. *Care for the interests of others.* I've told my wife that if I happen to precede her in death, I hope to have earned the following one-word epitaph on my grave marker—*Others.* I would like to have it said that I was consumed with a passion for showing love to others, investing in others, giving to others, sharing Jesus with others. I am mindful—and thankful—each week as I make preparations for Sunday morning that God has given me the privilege of declaring His Word and His truth to others. Be intentional about keeping people a priority as you live and as you lead.

3. *Live with integrity.* I heard someone say that integrity is what happens when the tongue in your mouth and the tongue in your shoes are all going the same direction—when what you say and what you do are in perfect alignment. Integrity carries the idea of wholeness, unity, and truthfulness. It means making each facet of your life worthy of emulation, not just those you want others to notice. Part of our high standard as leaders requires living in total integrity of heart.

4. *Keep your word.* If you tell someone you'll do something, do it. If you set a time to meet, be there—right when

you said you would. Jesus said to "let your word 'yes' be 'yes,' and your 'no' be 'no'" (Matt. 5:37). Don't say it unless you mean it. And mean it when you say it.

5. *Develop your gifts and potential.* Some people, even some leaders, feel exempt from risking the development of their talents. They fear the growing pains that are inherent in becoming all God designed them to be, the cost involved in maximizing their capacities and possibilities. Leaders can't afford to take that easy way out. It's always been my heart's cry to reach my God-given potential—not merely the one my church, my denomination, or my family expect of me but the one my Lord *knows* I can achieve, the potential He is continually equipping me to attain. We must let God do with His investment whatever He desires. He gave us these gifts and abilities for a reason. We must not waste a drop by lowering our standards.

6. *Manage well your time, talents, and treasures.* We know that time lost cannot be replenished. But we must not just retain this piece of information as knowledge; we must live it in real time. The leader must be alert each morning to the value of the day ahead. God has given you another package of hours to open and use. Look forward to what it may contain.

Talents—this makes me think of Jesus' story from the Scripture in which the landowner allotted talents to his servants: five to the first one, three to the next, then one to the last. I've always considered myself a one-talent person. I don't really have a lot of things I do naturally well. But the question is not how many talents we have; it is what we're doing with the talent we've been given. Take that one talent—even if it's just one—and spend it all for the glory of God's dear name.

Our treasures, of course, include our money and material possessions. By using and managing these well, we mere mortals, who can only be in one physical place at a time, can find ourselves multiplied—empowering others simultaneously in other regions of our nation and world. By investing our treasures, we can be giving and active even when we're asleep! But our treasures also include the people God has given us to share life with—our families and loved ones. Don't forget to invest deeply in them as well. Many a leader has set his sights on ministry and professional goals while losing sight of his responsibilities at home. Remember, leaders are held to a higher standard, and God will supply what you need to be as effective with your family as you are with your followers.

7. *Pass on to others what you have received.* One of the passions in my life is mentoring young pastors. For a good while now, I have been bringing one pastor a year (two pastors a year most recently) into a mentoring program at our church. The student must be a college graduate, must be studying for the pastorate, and be enrolled in seminary. I don't pay them much during this yearlong period, but I do give them a place to live, a large investment in their library, and a generous travel budget so they can go with me to various venues and see real ministry in action. Our seminaries even give them up to twenty hours credit for the time they spend with me.

Yes, this demands a lot of me as a leader. Investing in these young men takes me away from other things that could easily occupy my time on more pressing matters. But I know that if any of us ever amount to anything, it's because of what others have passed along and handed down—the investment they've made in our lives. I can only hope that these men will glean insights and lifelong memories that will be helpful to them down the line. It won't be what I *taught* them as much as what I showed them, not what they hear but what they see. Leaders must maintain this kind of forward thinking, making sure they are actively involved in efforts that will outlive them.

Perhaps your guiding principles should include some or all of these seven. Perhaps they should include others. But think of them all like a compass, fixing your bearings on true north, keeping you and your leadership goals magnetically joined, pointing in the same direction. They will narrow (and hopefully eliminate) any gap between what you consider important and what you actually spend your time doing. They'll help to keep *you* on track as well as your church, business, or organization. Guiding principles are must-haves in the leader's luggage.

Measurables in the Leader's Life

8

Progress is not an accident, but a necessity.

—HERBERT SPENCER

Someone will often ask a pastor or leader, "How's your church doing?" or "How's your ministry?" Our answer is almost always the same: "Things are going great!"

Junior Hill tells the humorous story of asking a pastor this very question, to which the man answered, "Things are really going great! It's never been this good before!"

"Wow, I'm glad to hear that," Junior said. "Tell me more about it."

The pastor replied, "I tell you, Junior, this church is dying slower than any church I've ever led."

"Yes, things are going great!" we say. We just hope they don't ask us how we *know* they're going great. What "going great" usually means is: "It hasn't fallen apart yet."

So if someone were to ask you today, "How's your church doing?" what would you use to determine if you're truly progressing? What measurables are in place to help you see how things really are? Are these facts your friends? Do you welcome this kind of truth in reporting?

At First Baptist Church, Woodstock, I measure our Sunday school growth and worship attendance against the same Sunday from the year prior. Comparing week to week is not particularly helpful because the numbers vacillate too much, depending on all kinds of variables. Looking at it a year at a time gives us a truer gauge of what's actually happening in our fellowship.

Not only do we measure vertically to see if we're heading in the right direction, but we also measure horizontally to see how people are getting involved in the work God has called us to do. Our goal is not merely to increase in number but also in quality, in relationships, and in true "life changes" across the board.

Here are eight of the measurables we use to monitor these objectives. Try adapting these to your own situation:

1. *Are you catching up to others who are ahead of you?* We look around at other churches to see what kind of job they're doing at reaching people—not to be envious or competitive but rather to be inspired by their success. The Lord wants us *all* to make a difference in our cultures and communities. So learning from others, drawing challenge from others, celebrating with others—it helps us be better at what we're doing ourselves. I think it's even healthy when various departments within the church are daring each other to perform at high levels. We never want to grow lax and lethargic, all habit and yesterday in our thinking. We dare not become

ingrown, only measuring ourselves against ourselves. God has created us to be motivated by others as well. Take advantage of this energy, drive, and hunger.

2. *Are you still feeling challenged in your work?* Each morning when I wake up, I'm aware that a challenge lies before me—the challenge to reach people, to be committed to both my neighbors and the nations in declaring the grace of God for fallen man. This is what God has called me to, and I want to be forever challenged by it. If I'm ever not, then I will know that I have stepped outside God's plan for me. I'll admit, I do sometimes get weary in the work, as I'm sure you also do. But after more than thirty years of ministry, I can say with gratitude to God that I have never grown weary *of* the work. May the tasks and needs of the coming day continue to fire us with the challenge of meeting them.

3. *Is your focus forward?* Your mentality should always believe that the best is yet to be. Never rest on your laurels. Never be totally satisfied with where you are. Always be looking ahead to the reality of what is yet to be done.

4. *Is the atmosphere affirming?* This is sometimes lost among other measurable components of your leadership success. But you and I should desire to create an environment that affirms those with whom we serve. Admonishments and corrections will always have to be addressed, of course, but life is too short for people to work within an oppressive, condemning environment. Affirm what God is doing in those around you, especially as it pertains to the big picture of what you're all doing together.

5. *Are you out of your comfort zone?* It's very easy to adopt a status quo attitude. Nothing is more natural and

inviting than the eight-lane highways of our own interests and expectations. But if we're going to reach our God-given potential, we must constantly force ourselves outside of our comfort zone, imagining what could happen if we tried something new. We must be willing to risk failure in order to attempt to do more.

6. *Are others giving?* I'm not just talking about money here, although money is definitely a part of it. As leaders, our lives should inspire others to want to invest in the purposes we espouse. Giving of ourselves wholeheartedly to the cause should spark a desire in our followers to join us on this journey.

7. *Is there a willingness to change?* Sometimes you will attempt something and it won't work. But that's not your only measurable way of determining how well you're leading. One of the key measurables of leadership is being able to admit a goof and to change it for the better, to spot the error and make the necessary adjustment. But this willingness to change shouldn't only apply to correcting areas in your work and ministry that are not getting results. A passionate leader will even take time to observe those initiatives that *are* producing fruit, implementing tweaks and enhancements that will help them perform at even greater capacity.

8. *Is growth being modeled and expected?* I've heard it said that if you want to grow your ministry, grow yourself. How devoted are you to the kinds of discipline that prepare you for leadership of others and submission to Christ? What are you recognizing in your own heart? We must be ever growing if we hope to see growth in the life of our people. There's no substitute for this kind of personal commitment.

As the quote at the beginning of this chapter says, "Progress is not an accident." Each of us should have a list of measurables that we constantly place before ourselves, keeping us challenged in our work, helping us ascertain when (and why) things are really "going great!"

The Insecure Leader 9

There is no such thing as absolute certainty, but there is assurance sufficient for the purposes of human life.

—JOHN STUART MILL

Insecurity can be quite natural in a leader. That doesn't make it something you can afford to put up with.

The insecure leader is the ultimate ministry headache. He is an active detriment to the church, placing both his work and his people in jeopardy, not to mention himself. That's because the very essence of leadership is "others." And the reason a leader is insecure is because he's thinking only of himself.

I know this sounds harsh. I know that not everyone responds to being spoken to so plainly, but I cannot emphasize enough the negative consequences of this attitude.

46

I hear from far too many leaders who suffer from it—and whose people suffer with them.

That's not to say I don't understand it. To admit that I had an inferiority complex early in my ministry would be the understatement of the new millennium. My college and seminary work exposed a lot of weaknesses and insecurities in me, which forced me to deal deeply with my self-doubts if I intended to remain on the course of my calling. I felt as though every other person was more qualified than I to serve in the capacity I was studying for. I was all set to become an insecure leader.

But as Solomon said, "Listen to counsel and receive instruction so that you may be wise in later life" (Prov. 19:20). The Lord put people in my path to remind me that He doesn't call the equipped; He equips the called. We each carry around our own load of insecurities, but they can all be handed over for Him to carry. That's how people who are insecure by nature become bold and confident by God's grace.

With this context in place, consider the following things that each of us need to know about ourselves as leaders—things that can help us lay aside our fears and inferiorities on the way to stable, steady leadership:

1. *You're a leader—act like one.* God has placed you in this position. So whether or not you feel like a leader on any given day, you are. And He will supply whatever is lacking. Ours is a position filled with privileges as well as incredible responsibilities. If we were to look only at the privilege part, we might consider ourselves more valuable than others. It's the responsibility aspect of leadership that weighs most heavily on our insecurities. And yet when I think of

the responsibility of leading others to Christ, helping them nurture their relationship with Him, I must consider even this a privilege. Own up to your many challenges. God will honor your efforts at being true to your calling.

2. *Leaders still have faults.* Facing down our insecurities isn't the same as declaring they don't exist. We should admit them, even as we're working to improve them. And one of the best ways to keep ourselves healthy and balanced in this area is by surrounding ourselves with people who can help us overcome our weak spots. If all we had to go on were our own perspectives, we'd never see ourselves as we really are. Place people around you who love and respect you but are not afraid to tell you the truth. The Bible says that the wounds of a friend are better than the kisses of an enemy (see Prov. 27:6). I want friends beside me who will be honest and up-front enough to help me develop into the best leader I can be—warts and all.

3. *Leadership amplifies your insecurities.* Don't be surprised by this. The minute you place your insecurity on the platform, it's in front of the whole group to see. No hiding. No wardrobe changes. No touch-ups and makeovers. There it is! But God has determined that this is something that needs to be dealt with, an area where He desires to show you how complete His empowerment of you can be. If He can help you do *this*—this thing that you know is impossible in your own strength, this obstacle that has kept you feeling insecure for as long as you can remember—He can help you do anything. Watching Him deal with your insecurities is one of the most painful but precious components of leadership.

4. *Insecurities grow larger as your organization grows.* I've known people who did an unbelievable job when leading a

church of three hundred members. But as their ministry doubled in size to six hundred members, the depth of their insecurities—which hadn't been pressed hard enough to crack before—caused them to collapse under the strain. When insecurities aren't dealt with, they only wait for another day to reveal themselves. And if you are leading a growing organization, the insecurities will eventually hinder you from reaching your greatest heights in reaching people. Face them now. Take away their damaging future.

5. *Insecure leadership is a lose-lose proposition.* Insecurity makes you unsure, which makes you indecisive, which bottlenecks the organization, which creates low morale, which stymies your productivity. Nothing good ever came of an insecure leader. If allowed to continue, you'll find it extremely difficult making the decisions that come before you each day, especially the hard calls. You'll lose the respect of your team and associates. You'll find yourself becoming more and more of a procrastinator. You'll be miserable at a job in which God intended to give you hard-fought, wholly fulfilling joy. Today is a good day to start changing the playing field—if you haven't done so already.

Insecure leaders? They don't stay leaders for long. The sooner you come clean, the sooner your capacity for greater things will come uncorked.

Spotting Insecurity 10

Avoid self-righteousness like the devil; nothing is so self-blinding.

—BASIL LIDDELL HART

I f you serve with an insecure leader, there's a good chance you've already noticed all these things we've been talking about, filing them away as clear evidence of what you're having to put up with. The trouble more often comes not in spotting these signs in others but in recognizing them in ourselves. For this reason I ask you to pay particular attention to the following symptoms of insecurity. They will give you ammunition for firing away at the parts of your own leadership style—and personal life—that are feeding unhealthy desires. Rather than working so hard to mask these things, wouldn't it be better just to do away with them altogether?

An insecure leader has a hard time giving credit to others. Andrew Carnegie said, "No man will make a great leader who wants to do it all himself or get all the credit for doing it." But insecure leaders have a burning need to be needed. Therefore, sharing the spotlight—giving credit where credit is due—feels like a subtraction from their importance rather than a multiplication of everyone's efforts. When others come up with great ideas, make sure they're recognized for it. When someone performs well, let him know. Even if it's something you thought up and asked him to do, the fact is—he did it! Why should praise seem like an unrecoverable cost? It is a gift that gives back to everyone.

An insecure leader keeps information from his staff. I've addressed this earlier in another context, but don't miss its connection to insecurity. Communication is a form of empowerment. When you release information, you convey trust and confidence to others. When you conceal it, you convey just the opposite: *no* trust, *no* confidence. The staff that surrounds you should be the very first people to hear any kind of vision you plan to cast to the whole church. By sharing with them first, you're not only letting them know how important they are to you, you're hopefully giving them an opportunity to shape the vision with their own unique insights and perspectives. Don't keep the circle so tight. Bring others into your private world, where all can contribute to your shared success.

An insecure leader doesn't want his staff exposed to other leaders—people who may possess qualities you don't, people who may have skills your staff wishes you had. When one person grows, your whole team grows. That's the way secure leaders see it. That's why, as John Maxwell says, "*A*s hire *A*s."

They are eager to bring the most talented, the most gifted, the most vibrant individuals into their ministries—workers who perhaps have more on the ball than even the leader does himself. But this is also why *B*s hire *C*s, why insecurity keeps a leader from surrounding himself with the most qualified staff members for fear that their light might dim the leader's, exposing a weakness no one had noticed before until they see how a truly capable person operates. Give your people the best—even better than *you* are.

An insecure leader is often a micromanager. He's a control freak. He feels the need to keep a tight rein on everyone—why?—so he can ultimately take the credit for everything. Therefore, nothing can happen on the campus, in the church, or (heaven forbid) in the worship service that the leader is not fully aware of. He has a hard time going on vacation, certain that things will fall apart without him around to hold them together. He'll probably even schedule an inferior communicator to preach so people won't get to liking something their regular pastor doesn't do. This kind of oppressive control wrings the life out of a church and ministry team. People need room for God to lead them in the direction of their own callings.

Insecure leaders are too needy of praise. For this reason, more than perhaps any other, they can't really be leaders. When someone needs his followers to always be telling him how wonderful he is, he works in direct opposition to the heartbeat of leadership, which is: building into others' lives. See if this concise statement registers with you: Secure leaders *love* people, but they don't need them. They will *be* there for them, but they don't require others to return the favor. They are secure enough in their calling and their open relationship with the Lord to need only His favor and blessing.

Insecure leaders don't provide security for those they lead. If the mood and environment in the office is one of fear, second-guessing, and self-doubt, you can be sure an insecure leader is in charge. Where the secure leader is free to appreciate and empower others, the insecure leader is hindered by the age-old truth that you can't give away what you don't have. People must be encouraged to feel good about themselves and what they're doing if you expect them to perform at high levels.

Insecure leaders take more than they give. Whether they realize it or not, they are on a personal quest for validation and affirmation. So instead of meeting these very real needs in others, giving them reason for confidence and encouragement, they are focused instead on receiving it. They are so hungry to draw up respect and compliments from the well of their own followers, they have little appetite for returning the favor. Secure leaders know that by watering the garden around them, they cause others to spring up and grow, opening up a world of new opportunities for the whole team.

Insecure leaders limit their best people. Secure leaders thrive on seeing others succeed, watching them attain the highest limits of their God-given potential, while insecure leaders cannot genuinely celebrate the victories won by others. How weak and cheerless it is to cling so tightly to one's own reputation, when holding on is keeping others from being their best. Secure leaders turn their most capable people loose and allow them to race forward at Godspeed.

Insecure leaders limit their organization. This is a corollary to the previous point but deserves to be mentioned on its own because it affects the entire scope of your ministry. Not only does insecurity throttle down the horsepower of individual team members; it results in putting restraints on the whole church or organization. That means people in the pew are affected. It means outreaches are short-circuited. It means those in need of God's help through God's people are left to suffer alone. Insecurity comes at a staggering cost. Hoarding away the whole group's potential is a sin not only against God but against everyone who loses by your futile attempt to gain affection and man-made affirmation.

I haven't meant to make you feel bad here. It's just that we all need to hear the nature of these threats, which are sure to become realities if we let our insecurities continue to run their unending course. Each of us is guilty of at least some of these errors, but we each have been given the empowerment of God to counteract them for His glory and for the health of our ministry. Therefore, may I match these nine statements with nine steps for fighting back against our fallen natures:

1. *Become vulnerable.* Confess your insecurity. Be honest, sincere, and transparent.

2. *Become accountable.* Give someone permission to be honest with you.

3. *Die daily.* Confess insecurity as a weakness, a sin, and ask the Lord to put it to death.

4. *Allow God to change you.* He is in the life-changing business, you know.

5. *Find your security and identity in Christ,* not in your service or position.

6. *Begin to praise recognizable achievement.* Actively look for opportunities to thank others.

7. *Allow others to get the credit by giving it.* None should have to take it. You should give it freely.

8. *Ask God to help you think clearly.* Insecurity is a form of confusion. Seek a convinced mind.

9. *Find a mentoring figure.* No matter how old we get, we can all use advice and encouragement.

Push hard to break through the stubborn will of insecurity. Imagine what horizons may yet be attainable if you approach them as a secure leader. 🔳

Being Ministry Conscious

11

To love or not; in this we stand or fall.

—JOHN MILTON

L et's say I'm on my way to the sanctuary on Sunday morning, where soon I'll be preaching God's Word to thousands of people. But as I'm walking down the hall, a lady approaches me and says, "God has answered my prayer. I prayed this morning that even though this church is so large, I might have the chance to speak to you personally." She then begins to tell me that she's just found out this week that she has cancer—an operable form, but cancer nonetheless. After sharing with her sympathetically for a few moments, I bow my head and ask God to minister His grace and blessings in her life.

My question for you as a leader is this: Will I do greater

ministry in this lady's life from the pulpit than I've just done in her presence?

We're of much more use to God before Sunday morning worship not huddled up in our studies putting the finishing touches on our sermon, but out among the congregation— looking, mingling, searching, listening—expecting ministry to happen.

I've often said that when a person is filled with the Spirit of God, he or she has the potential of accomplishing more "accidentally" than on purpose. It may be no more than a casual smile and a word of greeting to the person who's next to us at the gas pump. It may be as simple as catching your waiter or waitress's eye, not to ask for more napkins but just to say, "You're doing a wonderful job taking care of us." People are encouraged and attracted to those who speak words of blessing and affirmation into their lives.

Many times when I'm out to eat, I'll say to the server as our food is delivered, "Excuse me, I'm getting ready to bow my head and ask God's blessing on this food. Is there any-thing I can pray about for you or your family?" It is absolutely remarkable the responses I've gotten through the years. It has opened doors to build relationships that have later led to sharing Christ and seeing this person receive His salvation.

Remember, you can do ministry anywhere, everywhere.

I pray that God would give us the eyes of Christ to see the people we encounter today the same way He sees them. The world is full of hurting people. And if you will make it known that you genuinely care, it will be like raising a flag to announce that truth. Believe me, there will always be a large gathering around that pole, people who are desperate to be loved and listened to.

It's easy in this fast-paced world to find ourselves so consumed with our own needs and concerns that we don't slow down long enough to minister to others. But because of the way God works, always surprising us with His comprehensive care, it's remarkable how He will turn our acts of ministry into a means of ministry to ourselves. We benefit as much or more than the person we speak to or share with.

Jesus' disciples thought they were merely passing *through* Samaria the day He met the woman at the well—merely taking a rest stop and getting a bite to eat—but through this simple, by-the-way encounter, an entire city was introduced to the Messiah. It's a good reminder for us to be looking for opportunities everywhere. God often does His greatest ministry through us while we're on our way *to* our ministry.

The Day Moses Became a Leader

12

*One can remain alive long past the usual date of
disintegration if one is unafraid of change.*

—EDITH WHARTON

Most of us would think of Moses as one of the pre-
mier examples of leadership in all of human history.
Faithful to God, loyal to his people, somehow able to keep a
massive, nomadic nation intact for dozens of years. His biblical legacy is epic in proportion.

But there was a day—whether he had admitted it to
himself or not—when Moses' leadership was in danger of
collapsing under the accumulated weight of responsibility.
As strong a figure as he was, he could have barreled ahead
with bullheaded determination, confident from experience
that his way was still right. After all, it had been working

just fine up till now. But times were different. The dynamic of Israel's life had grown more complex. And if Moses was to continue as their leader, things needed to change.

Enter Jethro, the wise father-in-law of Moses. And observe Moses' reaction, which cemented his place in the leadership hall of fame. He was about to hear—and more importantly, realize—that his value as a leader would now depend not only on what *he* could do but also on what he could get done through others.

Exodus 18:17 records Jethro saying to Moses, "What you're doing is not good"—sitting from morning to evening each day, listening to the grievances of the people, attempting to mete out fairness and justice with mind and body growing increasingly fatigued. Things could not keep going on like this forever. Jethro could see it, even if Moses couldn't. "You will certainly wear out both yourself and these people who are with you," Jethro said, "because the task is too heavy for you. You can't do it alone" (Exod. 18:18).

Thank God for the principle and process of delegation. Jethro advised Moses that if he wanted to continue to be God's representative to the people—which he should—he needed to draw around him an able staff of godly men, assigning them to break up his caseload. This new organization would arrange the people in groups of thousands, hundreds, fifties, and tens, complete with a hierarchy of judges who could tend to these small groups and bring only the knottiest issues before the wise assessment of Moses. "If you do this," Jethro continued, "and God so directs you, you will be able to endure, and also all these people will be able to go home satisfied" (Exod. 18:23).

Many of you who are reading this book do not have a hired staff paid by the church. However, we all have the potential to surround ourselves with staff. In the early days of my ministry, the "staff" in my life consisted of a faithful group of laypeople who came alongside, like Aaron and Hur (see Exod. 17:12), to hold up my hands as I attempted to lead our little flock. We could never have done what we did without these wonderful people.

Perhaps, however, you find yourself in a much different situation. You have a number of paid staff members around you to care for the needs of the church. But your church has grown to that overload point where you're struggling with the fact that you can't be as personal with every single member as you used to be, the way you always wanted to be. Like Moses, it's probably time for a change of thinking. Like it or not, the leader of a church that's experiencing numerical growth will be forced to grapple with this dilemma. But rather than seeing this as a loss, realize (as Jethro advised) that this is best for both you and the people. In addition, never underestimate the marvelous ministry of intercession that can now be yours as the logistics of ministry adjust for you. You can serve as God's representative to advocate on their behalf—praying for them, building up the hedge, filling in the gap as you storm the gates of heaven with your intercessions on their behalf. God will do a much better job of caring for their individual needs than you can, using others on your staff and in your congregation to be the means of conveying His blessing.

Moses came to this point one day. He could dig in his heels and insist he was still up to the challenge of handling this alone. He could close his ears to Jethro's advice. He could stay blinded to the toll his leadership style was taking on himself, even on his people.

But Moses listened.

Moses—the great leader Moses—opted for change.

He "listened to his father-in-law and did everything he said" (Exod. 18:24).

We all form habits in life. Not all of them are bad habits, thank the Lord, but they are habits just the same. One of the difficult things about any kind of habit is that the longer it has room to settle into our hearts and our routines, the more difficult it becomes to change when life and wisdom call for it. A sign somewhere north of Anchorage, Alaska, makes this point even clearer. In a raw expanse of arctic land where the snow can grow deep and dense for long months at a time, the warning to vehicled travelers reads: "Choose your ruts carefully. You'll be in them for the next 125 miles."

Had Moses stayed in his rut, the people's demands would have eventually overrun his ability to meet them, sapping the energy he needed to stay open to God's direction, to stay fresh for the most needed and important aspects of his leadership. If you stay in the rut you're currently in, you too will fall prey to the well-worn motto: "If you keep doing what you've been doing, you'll keep getting what you've been getting."

Like Moses, is there something you're doing that is "not good"? Has a wise, older mentor given you counsel to change this or that way of approaching certain aspects of your ministry? Could it be that if you listen to him—and to the wisdom of God that may be speaking through him—

it will lead to a better result not only for you but also for everyone else?

Moses was faced with these same questions one day. He could have resisted. He could have stood pat. He chose instead to listen and to make the necessary changes for growth to occur.

It was the day that Moses truly became a leader.

Seven Changes That Make for a Better Leader

13

Very often a change of self is needed more than a change of scene.

—ARTHUR CHRISTOPHER BENSON

I t might seem best for *you*, but is it best for the people? That's the question Moses was forced to face after his encounter with Jethro. It's a question you, too, must face as the footprint of your leadership grows. That's because leadership is not about you; it's about helping others. And that makes this the kind of question that has a way of changing things. See what it changed in Moses' life—and what it may need to change in yours:

1. *Become a person of prayer.* We often say that prayer is important to us. But is it . . . really? We know the Bible

teaches that we ought to "pray always" (Luke 18:1), to "pray constantly" (1 Thess. 5:17), not to "worry about anything, but in everything, through prayer and petition with thanksgiving, let your requests be made known to God" (Phil. 4:6). But do we pray like that? Do we take to heart the words of Jethro to his son-in-law Moses when he admonished him to "represent the people before God and bring their cases to Him" (Exod. 18:19)?

I've learned over the years that I can't solve other people's problems. But God can. He's the answer regardless of the question. So every morning I pull up a prayer request sheet gathered each Sunday at our church, and I bring the needs of my people before Almighty God. I've found that the statement "I've been praying for you" is not an apology for being unable to do more. It is in fact one of the most meaningful acts we can do for others. But it does require change for many of us—moving away from being a person who thinks he must do it all himself, becoming instead a person who approaches the throne of grace as though he's on a mission. Truly we are . . . when we pray.

2. *Commit yourself to communication.* Being a teacher takes time. It takes discernment. It takes noticing what others need and knowing what to say. Moses was told to instruct the people in God's laws and decrees, to "teach them the way to live" (Exod. 18:20). But being faithful in this responsibility may require making some changes in your way of doing things.

Among the key changes involved in being a capable teacher is remaining currently teachable. One of the ways I do this as a pastor is by attending Sunday school. Many pastors choose not to be part of a regular Bible study class as a student, thinking they're too busy, that they're better off focusing on their sermons, that they're needed more urgently elsewhere. But I can say from experience that I am challenged weekly by my Sunday school teacher, Marty Benton. He calls me to go deeper, to think more broadly, to be serious about my obedience to the Lord. I can't count the times in my own teaching when I've referred back to something God has stirred in my heart during times at the feet of another.

You can't know it all, any more than you can do it all. If you want to be a better teacher of people—and you should—change your listening and learning habits. They are crucial to being a good communicator.

3. *Embrace and broadcast your vision.* There's more to leadership than teaching others "the way to live." As the last part of verse 20 says, we must also show them "what they must do." We must let them in on our dreams and goals. We must let them know—and be reminded ourselves—that they are a huge part of what is required to bring the corporate vision to pass.

I do this often from the pulpit, just speaking from my heart, talking with our people about the dreams God is birthing in me. I might say something like, "There's an available piece of land that seems ideal for us. It would give us room to enhance a certain ministry of ours. Being able to purchase it right now seems utterly impossible, but I want you to join me in praying about this, to see if it is indeed the Lord's will for us." We embark on this journey together, not in boardrooms and insider meetings. And if God chooses to make a way, then we celebrate the culmination together.

People cannot share a vision unless it's first been shared with them. But many leaders withhold this kind of information, afraid they'll only discourage people, shy about declaring big dreams in public that may sound too grandiose and out of reality. The God who gives the vision will invade it with His provision, but only as we allow Him to fulfill His purpose of letting the group embrace the effort. Remember, it's all about what we can do together under God's supply, empowerment, and direction, not what we can do ourselves. If you've become too ingrown and individual with your vision, be courageous enough to change this about your leadership style. Share it—and see the joyful results increase.

4. *Plan for the future.* As many as one hundred seventeen thousand people live within a five-mile radius of our church, nestled in a growing area north of Atlanta. Speaking of casting a vision, I have shared with our people a workable plan for knocking on each door in this swath of forty-five thousand houses, attempting to encounter every one of those one-hundred-plus people with the love of Christ. It's a big plan. It won't happen over one weekend. It won't be the kind of thing where we ask folks to meet at the church one Saturday morning, and we'll figure out what to do from there. Carrying out this God-sized mission to our community will take a great deal of preparation and planning. But if we're going to be obedient to Jesus' call to take the gospel to those within our "Jerusalem" (see Acts 1:8)—our nearest circle of influence— how can we leave it to happenstance and hope the doors just automatically open? There's nothing unspiritual about being serious enough to make a plan.

Is this a change you need to make? Have you let yourself become too dependent on things working themselves out, shooting in the dark and wishing for success? Plan for the future. Show people "what they must do."

5. *Select and train leaders.* When Jethro instructed Moses to "select from all the people able men, God-fearing, trustworthy, and hating bribes. Place them over the people as officials of thousands, hundreds, fifties, and tens" (Exod. 18:21), Moses began to pick out influencers. He looked for people who had the three major characteristics of leadership: morality, honesty, and integrity.

It's been said that leaders know leaders. But being on the lookout for new blood is a change that some leaders need to make. Don't let your ministry team grow stale and stagnant. Continue to flow new leaders into the bloodstream of your church or organization. When you begin calling to action those who display these three building blocks of leadership, you'll have people on the ball who are easy to train and capable of helping you take things to the next level.

6. *Turn ministry over to the people.* I like what Jethro advised in Exodus 18:22, referring to Moses' new leaders in training: "They should judge the people at all times. Then they can bring you every important case but judge every minor case themselves. In this way you will lighten your load, and they will bear it with you."

It does neither us nor our people any good if we raise up leaders but prevent them from actually leading. The purpose of selecting and training leaders is to turn them loose to lead, entrusting them with the deposit of wisdom and responsibility you've invested in them. It means taking your hands off the wheel that turns every ministry in your church, giving others some time in the driver's seat. And though it may go against your controlling tendencies, you're in for the ride of your life when you sit back and watch what God can do through others. It's a trip, let me tell you!

7. *Do what you do—what no one else can do.* Having matured to my current level of leadership, there are some things I don't have to do anymore. There's nothing I *won't* do, but some things are not the best use of my time as they once were. No one in our church can be me. No one in your organization can be you. Your day, week, month, and year will be populated by many things that only you can do.

Do it.

Moses knew what his father-in-law meant when he told him to have his assigned judges "bring you every important case" (18:22). Great leader that he was, Moses wasn't capable of being everything to everybody. But he was the only one called to handle the major matters of leadership. This called for focus, priority, and simplicity. It called for all seven of the changes we've discussed here. The reason you're not called to do everything anymore is not because you're too good to do it, but rather because it takes all you've got to do the few things well that only you can do.

Don't shirk your big responsibilities as a leader by staying good at the small stuff. You're needed for more—for championing the overall vision to your people. By making these changes, you'll see this vision embraced, encouraged, enhanced, and enlarged. You'll become the leader your people need.

And again, that's what really matters.

Leaders Need a Good Memory

14

Memory is a way of holding on to the things you love, the things you are, the things you never want to lose.

—Kevin Arnold

We talk sometimes about being able to reduce big ideas into manageable thoughts, into phrases and sentences that boil everything down to the basic elements, the heart of our message. The apostle Paul could summarize his sizable life experience in the space of eight words found in 1 Corinthians 15:10—"By God's grace I am what I am."

I'd call that a fitting description of all of us—wouldn't you?—all of us who keep our memories alive of where God once found us and what He's done for us ever since. We as leaders and followers of Christ cannot afford to forget what it was like to be lost, what it was like when we didn't know the peace and joy He brings to the human heart.

Where would we be without the Lord? I'm going to guess that, looking back, you can think of a whole lot of times when God's grace was all that kept you going. You were ready to give up, but He enabled you to persevere. You had made a huge mistake, but He saw you through to recovery. You were out of balance and totally overwhelmed, but He led you to Himself—the "rock" that is high above every mountain or obstacle (see Ps. 61:2).

God's grace, however, is more than a one-lane road from His storehouse to your door. He has found numerous ways of sending His grace your direction—through people who became part of His activity in your life, people who have prayed for you and invested their possessions into you over the years. As I share my own examples in this chapter, I encourage you to fill in the blanks with your own. These memories keep you grounded, balanced, able to paint a clearer picture of today by realizing how you got here.

Our congregation recently presented me with the address placard that once marked the home where I grew up in Wilmington, North Carolina. A few people had somehow heard that the government housing project where I spent my boyhood years was being torn down. And knowing of my past, they thought it would bless me to have these letters— 6-D Nesbitt Courts—as a memento.

It's hard to start much lower than I did. Raised by a single mom from the age of seven after my dad left home, I grew up on the mean streets. My mother worked two jobs—night and day—to make ends meet for my three brothers, two sisters, and me. I dropped out of school at sixteen, sure I already knew everything a guy needed to know, sure I didn't want to waste another day on books and learning. Thinking back to those years in the projects, being able to run my fingers across those old numbers again—they help to remind me how far God has brought me. How can you live a story like mine without feeling extremely humbled in heart? This is God's work. 6-D Nesbitt Courts is an address that people aren't supposed to outgrow. It's an address that has God's grace written all over it.

And prayers. Think of the people who have prayed for you. I think of the folks I met at Long Leaf Baptist Church in Wilmington, where I began to attend as a twenty-year-old. They could see my tears during the worship service. They knew the Lord was working hard on me. And on January 7, 1973, when Jesus Christ changed my life forever, they knew I was only beginning to need their prayers for God to help me, use me, bless me. My mind is flooded with memories even as I write this—the faces of so many people who interceded for me on a regular basis. I am what I am because of God's grace and His people's prayers.

In addition to their prayers, several of these dear saints of God put their money where their knees were, making it possible for a know-nothing, know-it-all like me to go to night school to earn my GED, then to college for my undergraduate course work. Just getting in didn't mean much with no way to afford it. But with the recommendation of my pastor, Rev. M. E. Gibson, and the help of a gentleman named Felton Baker, who withdrew money from his own retirement and savings to make my first payment at Gardner-Webb College, I was off and running on God's call to become a minister.

I think of Howard and Isabel Carter, who owned the skating rink next to our church—a couple I had often cursed at and reviled as an unsaved teenager prowling their establishment—now seeing the grace of God on my life and giving their own money to help support me at school.

I think of Otis and Viola Scruggs, a couple that God placed in my life during the college years. Both of their boys had died in childhood, victims of kidney diseases. But God had given this faithful man and wife a burning desire to be the parents of a preacher, and they poured every bit of that passion into me, investing their love and possessions into my life. They helped pay my tuition, bought clothes for my family and me, took us out to eat more times than I can recall. Many times when they would shake my hand, it would come with a twenty-dollar bill inside, just to help us out.

I think of Bob and Nancy Peeler. Bob was a deacon at Lavonia Baptist Church, my first church to pastor while still a college student. They cared for us financially and encouraged me as a young minister. The Lord only knows all the ways this couple invested in me, believed in me, became a vehicle of God's grace toward me.

I think of Z. O. Cobb, an older gentleman I led to the Lord. He and his sweet wife, Helen, bought us necessities, babysat our children, tended to us like we were their own. Their names unite with so many others who saw what God was doing in me and rushed to be part of His gracious activity. If you're one of these who has invested so generously in my life with your prayers, your time, your counsel, your encouragement, your dinner table, your financial help, your patience, your unconditional love—know that you are dearly and deeply loved.

And remembered.

Yes, I remember. Leaders need a good memory. As you spend some time today rifling through your mental files of people who have been there for you along the way, thank God at their memory. Realize all the ways He has kept you from falling by His grace, sending you the right individuals at just the right time to uplift and support you, to believe in you.

If you ever see a turtle on a fence post, you'll know he didn't get there all by himself. And whenever you look in the mirror or pull up deposits from your memory bank, you should see yourself as a person who "is who he is" by the grace of God alone. You can't afford to be a leader any other way.

Never forget.

Leaders Need Encouragement 15

Flatter me, and I may not believe you. Criticize me, and I may not like you. Ignore me, and I may not forgive you. Encourage me, and I will not forget you.

—WILLIAM ARTHUR WARD

As leaders, we certainly cannot let others' opinions of us govern the way we feel about ourselves and our mission. But let's not be stoic enough to say that we are immune from needing encouragement. This is not a sign of weakness or a soft spot in our character. Sometimes we just need to be told that what we're doing is good, that it's significant, and that we're making a difference. Not a single thing wrong with that!

Read the apostle Paul's letters, and you'll see that he was often thanking those in the churches for their encouragement and support of his ministry. Oh, he definitely knew how to shoulder persecution. He was no stranger to calls for his head and threats to his work. He bravely depended on God when things got tough. But Paul—that great leader of the early church—also depended on the reinforcements of his friends.

Perhaps that's why near the end of his life he took the time to write young Timothy—to pass along the kind of encouragement Paul knew was invaluable in a leader's life. Remember, Paul was Timothy's father in the faith. He even referred to Timothy as his beloved son, his "dearly loved child" (2 Tim. 1:2). Paul was in prison, awaiting execution—a thought that must have cut the young pastor Timothy to the core of his being. This man who had mentored, led, and pastored him was about to be gone. No longer would he be there to answer his questions, share his concerns, and give him counsel.

Leave it to a wise leader like Paul to know that what Timothy needed in that hour was to know what he meant to his spiritual dad.

The term Paul used in referring to him as his "dearly loved child" is the strongest possible word for *love* in the Greek language. Filled with the Holy Spirit, Paul poured out the love of God on his young protégé, ministering to his heart as few other expressions could do. Love and appreciation have that kind of effect on a leader, and we shouldn't apologize for it—because when we're leading as we should, what others love in us is really what the Lord is doing through us.

I was reminded of this humbling fact one Sunday morning while greeting guests during our time of reception after the 9:30 service. A former member at our church who had relocated to another state had made a special trip that weekend to be with us in worship. She had come with her teenage daughter on a mission, with a unique objective in mind.

As the room began to clear and I was preparing to leave, this woman, along with her daughter, walked over and said that she had been impressed while praying for me that week to come tell me how much our ministry had influenced their family. I remembered her and her husband being a great blessing when they were actively involved in our fellowship, and she wanted to be certain I knew that we had been a tremendous blessing to them as well.

By this time no one was present but the three of us. Everyone else had filed out. That's when she told me that the Lord had placed Romans 10:15 in her heart that week— "How shall they preach, except they be sent? as it is written, How beautiful are the feet of them that preach the gospel of peace, and bring glad tidings of good things!" (KJV)—and that He had given her (she felt) an unusual assignment. She asked if she could honor the Lord's instruction by demonstrating her love to me in this yet unspoken way.

Again, if it was just about me, a man could take this the wrong way. But I knew in my heart that she was motivated by her deep love for Jesus, and I said to her that I could want nothing more than for her to be obedient to Him.

At that, she asked if I would remove my shoes. I did. She knelt down in front of me, bent her face to the ground, and gently kissed both of my feet. Then she stood up and thanked me for the "beautiful feet" that had brought her and her family the gospel.

I will never forget that unexpected act of affection and kindness. It reminded me of why I do what I do—why God called me and prepared me for Christian ministry. To realize that something as unappealing and unattractive as my own two feet could become in God's hands an instrument of blessing was a staggering moment of encouragement.

I remember another time—just a typical Saturday afternoon—when I had performed a wedding ceremony at our church and was walking across the parking lot, preparing to leave. I noticed that a van had parked right next to my car. And as I drew closer to it, a young girl—Heather—around ten years of age, stepped out and addressed me. In her hand was a small red ribbon with the inscription, "You made a difference."

She told me that her schoolteacher had handed out these ribbons to their class that week and had challenged the students to give them to people who had significantly impacted their lives. Heather reminded me—right there between her family's vehicle and mine—how the Lord had used me to lead her father, then her mother, and later her sister to Christ. Heather, too, had received Jesus as her Savior under my ministry. The person she wanted to give her ribbon to—the person who had "made a difference" in her life—was me.

That Saturday afternoon was at least twelve years ago. But again, I've never forgotten it. The love, affection, and encouragement of others has that kind of staying power, even in the heart of a big, strong leader.

We need it. And that's OK. We can't be dependent on it, but we can be appreciative of it. In fact, it would probably be a good idea right now for you to sit back and recall the people who have literally been blessed of God because you came into their life. This is not an attempt to arouse your pride or ratchet up your self-righteousness. But you surely know—as I do—that our enemy has no issue with leaning hard on us, making us think we'd be better off throwing in the towel. It helps to remember sometimes how many people love and care for us deeply. They love us for who we are . . . and for who we're not. They love us for what God does in their hearts through our example and ministry. And I pray that the Lord would bring them tenderly to your mind this day, overwhelming you with His encouragement, refueling your enthusiasm for serving Him.

Go ahead. Feel the love. Be renewed in others' affection.

Leaders Need Prayer

16

More things are wrought by prayer than this
world dreams of. Wherefore, let thy voice rise like
a fountain for me night and day.

—ALFRED, LORD TENNYSON

Truly we will be short-circuited in every area of life if we are not praying people. But just as we can tend to neglect our *own* discipline of prayer, letting it slip into mere functionality, becoming little more than mealtime and bedtime (and crisis time!) prayers, so we can also discount the value of others' praying for us. Perhaps we may ask offhand for folks to lift us up in prayer, knowing that's the religious thing to say. And yet we oftentimes can be guilty of not really meaning it, not being utterly convinced that we are dependent on what God does through the petitions of others on our behalf.

Petition. That's what I like to call it. It's what Paul assured Timothy he was doing for him as a young pastor and leader: "I thank God, whom I serve with a clear conscience as my forefathers did, when I constantly remember you in my prayers night and day" (2 Tim. 1:3).

Paul not only loved Timothy, he lifted him to the Lord—not because it was the spiritual thing to do or say, but because he knew (from his own very real, very dangerous experience) that others' prayers were absolutely essential for a leader.

I've referred to this biblical account before in the book, but I think of it often in terms of prayer. You certainly remember the well-known passage in Exodus 17 that tells about the Israelites' battle with Amalek. Moses positioned himself along with his associates Aaron and Hur on a hill overlooking the fighting: "While Moses held up his hand, Israel prevailed, but whenever he put his hand down, Amalek prevailed. When Moses' hands grew heavy, they took a stone and put it under him, and he sat down on it. Then Aaron and Hur supported his hands, one on one side and one on the other so that his hands remained steady until the sun went down" (vv. 11–12).

The praying of our people for me does exactly the same thing. I know it! The Lord knows the times when my arms have grown weary in ministry, when I've felt myself weakening under the load of responsibility and the battle for peoples' souls. We all experience it. *You* experience it, no matter what kind of group God has called you to lead. The prayers and encouragement of others become for me like the strong arms of Aaron and Hur, bracing themselves up under me, coming to my aid, allowing me to rest on the steady support they provide. I need it. You need it. We need their prayers! My sincere desire as a leader is to continue to live close and clean—so that when the Lord Jesus calls me home, He'll be able to say, "Johnny, your hands were steady until the going down of the sun."

Prayer can make this a reality.

Can you imagine having someone of the caliber of Paul—the great apostle Paul—praying for you night and day? What encouragement that must have been in the life of young Timothy.

I remember one day when Fred Wolfe called me on the phone. At the time he was still pastor of Cottage Hill Baptist Church in Mobile, Alabama—a large, vibrant fellowship that has seen thousands come to Christ through their presence and outreach in the community. He remains the pastor emeritus of that congregation. Fred is known as a "pastor's pastor," a respected leader who has held many key posts in our denomination. Both he and his ministry have long been bigger than life to me. You can imagine my utter surprise, then, when I heard him say to me on the phone that day, "Pastor Johnny, I just want you to know that the Lord has placed it in my heart to pray for you. And by the grace of God, I will pray for you for the rest of my life."

Wow!

On another occasion I was making my way through the Atlanta airport when I happened to pass Henry Blackaby, a man I respect a great deal. As soon as we'd spotted each other, he approached me and asked: "Well, how is the pastor doing that I pray for every morning?" I'm telling you, that overwhelmed me, like a lightning bolt to the chest. God arrested my attention. Just think, this man whom I believe hears from God—more clearly than most anyone else I know—has been interceding for me daily at the throne of grace. What an encouragement!

Oh, the list could go on and on. God only knows the hundreds who receive my prayer e-mail every month, people all over America and in many countries around the world who are praying for me. What a mess I would be without them!

Don't try to be an effective leader without making sure you have lots and lots of good prayer support, people who are going to God on your behalf, asking Him to intervene in your life, and to use you for His awesome glory. If you want the sky to be your limit, you need people around you who know how to rise above the earth's gravity and take your cause into the heavenlies, the same way you do for them.

Leaders
Need Respect

17

I'm not concerned with your liking or disliking me.
All I ask is that you respect me as a human being.

—JACKIE ROBINSON

I n the last couple of chapters, we've looked at the leader's
need for encouragement as well as his need for prayer.
But an honest evaluation of this subject would be incomplete without admitting this one other need on the leader's
list: the need for respect.

And like most everything else of importance in his life,
the best source of respect comes from home.

Show me a leader who is forced to go outside his family
to find someone to respect him, and I'll show you a person
who's only half the man he could ultimately be. Respect
is something that's nice to have from others, but nothing

comes close to topping the respect a husband receives from his wife. The Bible is quite plain and to-the-point about this: "To sum up, each one of you is to love his wife as himself, and the wife is to respect her husband" (Eph. 5:33). It's hard to be much clearer than that.

My wife Janet and I have been married nearly forty years. And as I think back through the life God has graciously allowed us to enjoy together, I can say with all frankness that my wife has been the model of respecting her husband. I remember so many times when something exciting would happen to me in the course of a day—some opportunity that had arisen, some privilege or honor I had never dreamed in a million years would be mine to participate in. I'd call home to tell Janet about it, enthusiasm rippling through my voice. She'd say, "I'm really happy for you, honey, but I'm not surprised. I always knew God would use you like this." She's just always believed in me.

I hope you enjoy that kind of respect from your wife. I hope you're serious about *earning* that kind of respect from her. If you need someone to remind her how important this need is in your life, take this book to her, open it to this page, and let me do the talking: "Dear sister, this man will be more for you than you ever imagined when he rides on the wings of your respect. I promise you."

(Now you go do your part: loving her the way Christ loved the church. That'll keep you too busy for any moping or complaining.)

But ideally for a leader, respect needs to come from a wide range of quarters. Paul gave Timothy respect, and it meant the world to him. When Paul complimented Timothy on his "sincere faith" (2 Tim. 1:5), he was saying in essence,

"When I think of you, Timothy, I think of someone who is completely genuine and unhypocritical." He had seen enough of Timothy to admire what he observed in him, and he was eager to let him know of the high regard in which he held his young "son" in the faith. The language of that verse gives the impression that Paul was certain, utterly convinced, and had no doubt in his mind that Timothy was the real deal. Paul had great respect for this faithful pastor—a fact that must have filled Timothy's sails when he read and pondered it.

Just imagine what Timothy must have felt like the first time he heard Paul refer to him in terms like these: "Now you, man of God, run from these things; but pursue righteousness, godliness, faith, love, endurance, and gentleness" (1 Tim. 6:11).

A "man of God." Paul called me a "man of God"!

Everyone needs somebody to believe in them. And when that somebody was the apostle Paul—a man who didn't toss out free compliments like lollipops at a Christmas party—when Paul felt you'd earned the right to be commended for your example and leadership, his "man of God" statement meant something. My, that must have set Timothy's heart ablaze with enthusiasm!

In my early days of ministry, I got to where I was *almost* comfortable in the little pulpit God had called me to fill. But when I would be invited to speaking engagements outside of that particular church setting, I'd find myself extremely nervous and uncertain. I'd cry out to God in desperate dependence, "Lord, if you don't help me, I'll fall flat on my face when I go out there today." I remember my first opportunity to speak in a theological seminary environment.

I had been invited by the president of Mid-America Baptist Theological Seminary, Dr. Gray Allison, to come address their chapel service. I can still remember how little I slept the night before, scared to death of standing before the faculty and student body and all the gathered scholarship in that room. I prayed that God would use me to speak into their lives, but I still quaked in my boots at the thought.

No doubt it was God Himself who took over that morning and proclaimed His Word through me. People ask me sometimes, "How do you know when you've got the touch of God on you in the pulpit?" I answer, sad to say, "Because I've stood behind that sacred desk too many times when I *didn't* sense it, when I've tried to pull it off on my own." But oh, that day at the seminary, God showered me with His precious anointing, and His message reached into the hearts of many in attendance.

After the service as I was speaking to various people who had gathered around, one of the almost legendary professors at that great institution came up to me—Dr. Roy Beaman, professor of Greek, now retired from duty and home with the Lord. The seminary president himself had studied Greek under Dr. Beaman, as had my beloved mentor, Adrian Rogers. Knowing that a man like Dr. Beaman had been in the auditorium listening to me, following along in his Greek New Testament, was one intimidating thought to behold.

As he and I were talking, one of his students passed close by, interrupting us a little by asking, "Dr. Beaman, did Pastor Johnny light a fire in your heart today?" I'll never forget the passionate words of that dear man of God as he turned to his young pupil and said, "No, son, Jesus lit the fire in my heart many years ago, but God used Johnny Hunt to fan the flame of that fire in a marvelous way today."

Oh, to hear such words of respect from a man I greatly admired—much as Timothy must have felt to hear the apostle Paul commend him for his work and ministry.

"Don't neglect the gift that is in you," Paul had said to him before (1 Tim. 4:14). "I remind you to keep ablaze the gift of God," he now brought back to his attention again (2 Tim. 1:6). This bold apostle knew God's calling when he saw it on a man. He knew when that person was eagerly embracing it, totally committed to the faithful fulfillment of his ministry duties. He respected Timothy for what he had been, what he was, and what he was becoming. And that respect energized Timothy like few other things possibly could.

Thank God for those who respect you and your leadership role and who don't mind telling you so. Receive their compliments and words of support as gifts to God, sent by way of your delivery box. But as you're rerouting the praise of men to its rightful recipient—to the God of all grace—I don't think He would mind you enjoying the pleasant aroma and aftertaste. God knows we can use it to help us stay emboldened in our work as leaders.

Leaders Need Contentment

18

Do not spoil what you have by desiring what you have not; remember that what you now have was once among the things you only hoped for.

—EPICURUS

Part of what makes a leader effective is his dissatisfaction with the status quo, his willingness to make strategic changes rather than rest on his laurels. He must remain aware that the way things are cannot be the way they'll always stay—not if the enterprise wants to stay poised for future growth.

Having said that, it is also true that the restlessness he legitimately feels toward his organization's current modes and methods must be countered by contentment about his personal situation in life. A leader is equal parts of unsettledness and serenity.

So like the apostle Paul, we need to always be disciplining ourselves to say, "I have learned to be content in whatever circumstances I am" (Phil. 4:11). Contentment does not grow out of *accumulation* but out of *realization*—by realizing how good God has already been to us. We must always be grateful for what we have but never think we're too good to go back to what we used to have.

Some ministers are poor; some are wealthy. Some are in good health; some are not. Some are well rested; some are road weary; some feel encouraged today; some feel terribly discouraged and upset. As a pastor for many years, I can tell you that I've been underpaid, and I've been very well paid. I've been at challenging churches and cherished churches. I've been unappreciated and greatly appreciated. I've had enemies as well as close friends. To say that I've mastered the art of contentment would be saying too much, but God has taught me a lot and has helped me to grow in this area. I believe I can say in all honesty and humility that whatever my plight, I have learned to be happy in the Lord—whether living in a nice house or in the government projects. Can you?

I believe the secret of whole-life contentment is being happy in the following four areas:

1. *Your relationship with God.* Honestly, where are you right now in your daily experience with the Master? We should never be business-as-usual about that. Not only do we need to be present in the house of God, we need to be in the presence of the God of the house—daily, hourly, constantly. We know this, but is it a living reality for us,

our walk with our Savior? Nothing is more important than this.

2. *Your marriage.* Some people have fallen for the myth that marriage shouldn't be so much work. Some think that if they'd married the right person when they had the chance, they'd be having the life they always wanted. Some think that if they take care of their ministries, God will take care of their marriages. Some have simply conceded that marriage and ministry cannot stay in a manageable balance.

But did God not lead you into both—into your marriage as well as your ministry? Would He call you into a situation with the intended purpose of bringing unavoidable harm to either? Did He not establish both the family and the church (in that order, by the way)? Then you must be diligent to remain faithful in your marriage, to maintain friendship with your spouse, to stay flexible enough so that home life is not always given the short end of your attention. If you are not happy—not succeeding—in this one primary relationship on earth, you'll never stop having trouble in the less significant areas of life.

3. *Your ministry.* It's crucial that you're happy doing what God has called you to do. As a leader, you need to be settled in the knowledge that this is where God has placed you—at least for now—and that living in His will makes your current responsibility more satisfying than anything else you could possibly be doing. It's hard to get too excited about your work if it just feels like a job. But when you realize that this is your ministry—your God-given place of service for this season of life—it's nearly impossible to *keep* from getting excited about it. Give it your passion, bask in its purpose,

carry out the plan. Be happy wherever God has positioned you in His kingdom's work.

4. *Your money.* When the Spirit of God began convicting the Roman soldiers of John the Baptist's day through his preaching, some of them asked him, "What should we do?" In other words, how did John's message apply to the way they lived and operated, which was usually by looking for bribes, by cheating and intimidating people. John said, "Don't take money from anyone by force or false accusation; be satisfied with your wages" (Luke 3:14). Be content with what you have. Be happy, even if it doesn't seem like enough, even if others have more. Money is to be used and God is to be loved. You're banking on trouble if you get those two turned around—if you start using God and loving money.

Contentment is a key contributor to the freedom that's required for you to lead as God wants you to lead. You need to be happy and at peace with all four of these foundational areas of life. When you are, you'll then have the energy to shake things up in your church, business, or organization, to keep your vision moving forward. The ones who make the most headway are the ones who are the happiest where it counts.

The Secure Leader

19

To wish you were someone else is to waste the person you are.

—ANONYMOUS

Several chapters back we dealt with the issue of insecurity in a leader. I had more to say about it, but I wanted to take a little break—to blow a little space in here—before returning to it again.

My reason for investing so heavily in this topic is pretty simple: more leaders express to me their struggles in this area than in any other. Insecurity in leadership is a big deal. It's putting a choke hold on far too many good men and women, not to mention harming our collective work for the kingdom of God.

Many people want to lead, but few actually do. Many people *think* they're leading, but few actually are. Insecurity by its very nature is deceptive. It hides behind many layers of built-up, propped-up self-esteem, working behind the scenes to take us down, to render us irrelevant. In our unguarded, private moments, we know it's there. But because we're so reluctant to admit it—to deal with it head-on—we shove it back into its drafty corner, down where it does its dirtiest work in us and, by extension, in our churches and organizations.

The people who really see it in us are our families, our staff, and our colleagues. But who wants to be the first to tell an insecure person of his condition? How do you put it into words that don't set up an awkward, uncomfortable showdown? So insecurity often gets a free pass to roam under radar in our hearts, being present but not under pressure to be eradicated like the hideous enemy it is.

The next few chapters ahead concern what it takes to move from insecurity to confidence—in our leadership roles, in our relationships, in our discipleship. But to build the ground beneath us, I'd like to run one more diagnostic test to help you spot the holdouts of insecurity that need to be identified and targeted. Be open. Be honest. Your best days as a leader are still ahead, but not if these tendencies aren't stared down and knuckled under.

It could be said of insecure leaders that they have an "I" problem, as in the following nine attitudes:

1. *"I'm inadequate."* Not that we all aren't limited in various ways, but an oppressive sense of ineptitude or deficiency will strip away the lining from the strengths you *do* possess. A secure leader is not one who thinks he's invincible, but he's confident in what he can do. In guarding against overconfidence (which, of course, can lead to

stupidity), he doesn't swing into self-doubt and lose his self-assurance.

2. *"I'm inappreciable."* You may feel as though you're too small to be noticed or too far out in the middle of nowhere to make a significant difference. I've heard pastors of small churches in small communities confess this low estimation of themselves. Whoever you are, *wherever* you are, we all grow our churches and organizations one person at a time, no matter how large or how small our place of service. I promise, you can do something special from your current mailing address if you'll be courageous enough to look beyond your limitations.

3. *"I'm incapable."* One of the most encouraging elements to Christian living is that it's not what *we* bring to the table, but rather what God entrusts to us as we yield ourselves to Him. You may feel incapable of taking your church, business, or group where you'd love for it to go, but God is your supply. Don't downplay your Provider by considering His gifts to be discounted merchandise.

4. *"I'm incompetent."* More than a weakness of skill, this is the attitude that says you're not smart enough to pull off this endeavor, that you don't possess enough knowledge to do it well. In the biblical sense, knowledge is not the same as book learning. It is simply the wisdom and understanding that's accumulated through a lifetime of experience. As if that was not enough, God promises to give wisdom to those who seek Him for it. So as a Christian, you have an inside source for all the smarts it takes to lead others in a God-given vision. You are competent because He is your teacher.

5. *"I'm inconclusive."* One thing a leader must do is make sure he understands the vision he wants the people in his

organization to grasp. You will not be able to overcome a lack of clarity in your communication with others. Again, this doesn't mean you never question yourself or take time to analyze things. But once you've landed on a course of action, you move forward with confidence in your decision making. You build on beliefs that are unshakable. You settle on where you want to lead.

6. *"I'm incomplete."* So you're not what people would call the total package? Well, who is? We all need others around us to fill in the weaknesses and inadequacies we each possess. As mentioned earlier, however, this is where the real test of leadership comes into play. When you begin surrounding yourself with others who can share the load of leadership, are you threatened by their skills and personalities? Or are you thankful to God for people who are well trained and high capacity, people who may even be more gifted than you are? Until you can do that, you will never grow a sound, solid organization because it will always depend too much on one person—you. Be secure enough in your own skin to want others to succeed alongside you.

7. *"I'm inconsequential."* You have been called of God to live a significant life. You are important enough to Him to be filled with talents, to be placed on mission, to be assigned a role in His kingdom. Do not let a whiny sense of insecurity take away what God has so carefully and intentionally invested in you. You matter. You bear a significance born of your Savior's love and grace. Live it. Lead with it.

8. *"I'm inferior."* One of the most haunting realities of insecurity is the futile attempt of constantly comparing yourself with others. Did you see the quote at the beginning of this chapter? That's a statement worth waking up to

each morning. Look, you've got too much important stuff to accomplish to be wasting time worrying how you stack up against your coworkers, your friends, or (for goodness sake) total strangers. Seek to be who God created you—*you!*—to be. Make it your life's goal to reach your personal, God-given potential.

9. *"I'm inhibited."* It's always easy to blame your problems on others, on the someones and somethings that seem to be holding you back. Barriers and roadblocks are definitely real, but they are obstacles to be overcome, not excuses for failure. No one ever made a go of leadership who stopped just because the path wasn't clear ahead of him. You're not inhibited by life's challenges; you're inhabited by the Spirit of the living God!

Each of these nine evidences of insecurity breed dysfunction and confusion in the church. Secure leaders, however, have the potential of breeding clarity and confidence. It's what you owe to your people. It's what you owe to yourself.

The Secure Leader's Relationships

20

The greatest good you can do for another is not just to share your riches but to reveal to him his own.

—BENJAMIN DISRAELI

L eadership, like all of life, is really about people—relating to people, encouraging people, helping people, better-ing people. The Bible points up the folly of pouring ourselves into things that rust, rot, and decay. What better way to avoid the waste of such worthless pursuits than by using your leadership influence to build into the lives of others, those who by God's grace and design are eternal by nature.

But the health of these relationships will always be in direct proportion to your own sense of security. How can you enjoy beneficial relationships with others if you constantly feel incomplete and inadequate in yourself? The secret to being effective in working with others, leading them to embrace and employ the gifts of God in their lives, is being confident with what God is doing in yours.

With this in mind, consider the following five attributes of the secure leader. Ask yourself what it would take—what needs to be added in, what needs to go—in order for your leadership style to embody these liberating traits:

1. *A secure leader believes in others.* Rather than requiring a feeling of superiority in order to hold his head up, a secure leader only increases in confidence when those around him succeed and become more secure themselves. They derive no pleasure from seeing others going underchallenged or kept under wraps. The secure leader's desire is to see as many people as possible released for viable and effective ministry. They want for others what they want for themselves.

The Bible says that God has appointed leaders in His church "for the training of the saints in the work of ministry, to build up the body of Christ" (Eph. 4:12). Leaders are in the reproductive business, getting other people involved, inspiring them to believe in themselves and in the work God has called them to perform.

But it's nearly impossible to believe in others when you don't even believe in yourself. And when you don't have confidence in *others*, you can't encourage them in a genuine way. Work to develop a greater capacity for believing in what God can do through the people around you, no matter where they are in life or how you begin things with them. Believe in what you can do to help them. Want nothing more than to see them satisfied in their various stations of service.

2. *A secure leader loves people.* When your focus is not on yourself, when you're not so worried about how

a relationship will benefit you personally, you are freed up to love others more unconditionally. This leads me to make a statement that I hope you don't take the wrong way: when you feel genuinely loved by someone, it's not so much a reflection of how they view *you* but rather how they view themselves. Since they are not particularly into their own persona, reputation, or appearance, they are able to direct that energy into authentic love and appreciation for others.

If you are bottled up with insecurity, your relationships are much more likely to be governed by fear—fear of being one-upped, overshadowed, taken advantage of. But as the Bible says, "There is no fear in love; instead, perfect love drives out fear, because fear involves punishment. So the one who fears has not reached perfection in love" (1 John 4:18). It is hard to love people we're afraid of. It's hard to want the best for someone who is perceived as a threat to us. Gaining security as a leader will alleviate the needless effort we expend to protect ourselves, helping us choose instead to seek the hearts of others and guide them toward their God-inspired goals.

3. *A secure leader engages others for others' sake.* Insecurity begets self-centeredness. All activities are done with the underlying purpose of benefiting number one. But a secure leader wants others to succeed so that the person himself, the person herself, can gain confidence and grow in their usefulness to God, the church, and others. As I said before, the secure leader isn't even worried that this person might be better at what he or she does than the leader is himself. If so, great! That'll make the work we do together even more effective than before. Isn't that the whole point?

I can't say this enough: as a leader, your focus must be on others—who they are, what they need. This is not only true in building a church or some other corporate entity but also in building a home, building a marriage, building a family. When your focus is deliberately on others, you make it a priority to meet their needs. You help them grow into healthy, secure people who are in turn a blessing to you. Everybody benefits.

4. *A secure leader doesn't have to win.* Perhaps nothing exposes insecurity like the fear of failure. This seems to be especially predominant in churches where pastors and other leaders are often paralyzed by the prospect that something they attempt may not fly. Instead, they resort to a pattern of sameness or a prayerless reluctance to step out of their comfort zones, even on orders from the Spirit of God to do so.

Losing is a part of life. Cast enough visions, champion enough dreams, try enough new ideas, and you'll eventually sponsor your share of flops. But when it happens—as it inevitably will—the secure leader doesn't take it as a personal affront, doesn't get his feelings hurt, doesn't receive it as a rejection of his ministry. He simply figures that he may have stepped out in error, admits his failure, trusts that God will bring something profitable to pass from the effort anyway, and tries leading it in the proper direction. We're not perfect. We can't win 'em all. The secure person can be happy with that . . . without going into a tailspin of self-doubt and surrender.

5. *A secure leader can be himself.* Since God only makes originals, why do we work so hard to be a copy? There are certainly people worth emulating, just as Timothy strived to emulate the faith and ministry passion of the apostle Paul.

But God has placed within each of us originality, along with the engine of creative productivity to fire our unique identities into practical expression. Secure leaders have no trouble being themselves. They know it's a lot less work than trying to be somebody they're not.

When was the last time you gave yourself a day just to consider some of the ideas and dreams that God has placed within your heart? Imagine what might be born and brought to life as a result of letting Him reveal to you what He's purposed and planned for you to do? It's only the secure leader who can become like a pioneer trailblazer, burning a path that others can follow. What might that look like in your life if you let it happen?

I know that we stand on the shoulders of those who have gone before us. I know we follow in a long line of witnesses who have faithfully led God's people in the past. But when my life is over, I do not wish to look back and see that I have only marched down trails someone else had blazed years ago. I pray that I'll be able to see my own footprints as the first ones making tracks in some of the paths God laid before me, inspiring growth and success in others as He led through me.

There is a walk, a gait, a graciousness that insecurity can only limp through at best. It takes a secure leader to walk believing in God, believing in himself, and believing in those that God has placed alongside to assist on the journey. Just as insecurity starts with *i* and ends with *y*, the *u* in the center of security is its drive and priority—its focus on *you*, on others. As secure leaders, we're just glad to be together on our journey to God's best.

The Secure Leader's Discipleship

21

The strength of a man's virtue should not be measured by his special exertions, but by his habitual acts.

—BLAISE PASCAL

There's no way to keep insecurity from eventually becoming a drain on your character. Everything that goes into making a leader insecure—his self-centered focus, his emphasis on appearance, his fear of being outshone, his constant comparing with others—all of these war against the key components of virtue.

Honesty and integrity don't grow in a heart that's accustomed to believing lies. Boldness and exhortation don't spring forth from people who are convinced they're inadequate and incomplete. The great hallmarks of Christian character are dependent on a person's ability to stand firmly in God's grace and to live with wholehearted, undivided devotion. Wherever insecurity is given the chance to clog up the free flow of affection and authenticity, a leader's life and mind-set become too complex and complicated. He's unable to run unhindered. There's too much standing between him and genuine discipleship.

So I want to offer a handful of tips for helping you gain security within yourself. By contributing to your excellence in character, these can't help but increase your leadership potential:

1. *A secure leader remains teachable.* I've touched on this before, but it cannot be overstated. None of us ever reaches the place where we can't continue to learn. Heaven help us if we think we do. Paul instructed Timothy, "Take heed to yourself and to the doctrine" (1 Tim. 4:16 NKJV). That little phrase—*take heed*—appears nearly five dozen times in the Bible, almost always referring to someone's need to take personal responsibility for his character and understanding. Remaining teachable is an imperative in the leader's life.

2. *A secure leader continues to grow.* I have found growth to be the direct result of three things: discipline, time, and intentionality. None of these words or concepts can be discounted in leadership. Just as discipline in diet and exercise is essential to maintaining physical health, discipline in all areas is required for us to grow to the heights God aspires for us. Stewardship of our time, likewise, will cause the caliber of our leadership either to rise or fall, almost in direct proportion to our diligence in this important matter. And intentionality—when I stand to preach God's Word, I do it with the clear intention that God desires to communicate an element of His truth to our people. A secure leader does

few things without intentionality. He can afford to risk, is confident in his overall endeavor, and can walk assured that the character God is growing within him will guide him rightly.

3. *A secure leader inspects his own growth.* This is accomplished with the time he saves from inspecting the growth of others. Rather than sending his thoughts off on continual errands to see how the rest of the crowd is doing by comparison, the secure leader can sink his evaluation efforts into monitoring his own development, priming himself for ever greener growth—growth that the insecure leader doesn't think he needs. Paul asked the self-righteous religious people, "You then, who teach another, do you not teach yourself?" (Rom. 2:21). The secure leader takes seriously the patterns and habits of his own life, not excusing weaknesses in character but holding himself to standards set by God alone. He knows because the Lord is within earshot, thanks to His indwelling Holy Spirit, this leader can stay instructed in God's ways, always positioned for the future.

4. *A secure leader stays mentally sharp.* I couldn't say this any better than pastor and author Gordon MacDonald said when speaking on mental flabbiness:

> In our pressurized society, people who are out of shape mentally usually fall victim to ideas and systems that are destructive to the human spirit and human relationships. They are victimized because they have not taught themselves how to think, nor have they set themselves to a lifelong pursuit of the growth of the mind. Not having the facility of a strong mind, they grow dependent upon the thoughts and opinions of others. Rather than dealing with ideas and

issues, they reduce themselves to lives full of
rules, regulations, and programs.

Again, an insecure leader is unable to admit his need for
this kind of discipline or doesn't trust that he's got what it
takes to grasp big concepts. A secure leader doesn't let what
he doesn't know become an excuse for continuing to stay
ignorant.

5. *A secure leader is a giver, not a taker.* He doesn't grow
just to fatten his influence but to share what God is doing
in his heart. He doesn't look on expansion as a tribute to his
sizable abilities but rather as a way to do more good for more
people, to contribute more effectively to the work of God
in additional people's lives. Looking at the second part of
1 Timothy 4:16—a verse mentioned earlier in this chapter—
Paul told Timothy the reason why he was exhorting him to
"take heed" to growing in knowledge and understanding:
"for by doing this you will save both yourself and your hearers." The insecure leader doesn't have the emotional energy
to think this much about another's benefit. But persevering
in growth has an inspiring objective for the well-balanced
leader, giving him the opportunity to invest renewable
energy into the lives of those he serves.

6. *A secure leader asks lots of questions.* Two of my life
mentors have gone home to be with the Lord in recent
years, but among the most inspiring qualities of my friends,
Dr. Jerry Falwell and Dr. Adrian Rogers, was their eagerness
to seek wisdom from others. I don't remember a single time,
while attending board meetings for Dr. Falwell's Liberty
University, when he didn't pull me aside to ask about our
ministry or about my opinion on some matter of ministry.
He craved the insights of others, gleaning what he could to

enhance his stewardship of all that had been placed under his responsibility. Dr. Rogers, as well, after retiring from Bellevue Baptist Church in Memphis, Tennessee, was preparing to use his many years of experience to train and equip other pastors. Many was the time my phone would ring, and it would be Adrian Rogers, asking me questions about how I conducted my Timothy+Barnabas school. I can say with absolute, firsthand assurance—and you would hardly be surprised to hear—that these two men of God were among the most secure Christian leaders of our generation. Yet they were voracious about asking questions and getting better at what they did.

That's the kind of leader I strive to be—always seeking to learn, to grow, to improve, always assured that the best is yet to come. I've heard some pastors say jokingly, "My next sermon will be the best I've ever prepared." I hope in my case that this sentiment is true.

I want to constantly get better at what God has entrusted me to do, growing in my capacity to serve Him and to serve others. We can never be known as secure leaders until this is our heart's desire, until we're as willing to admit our need for help as we are to put what we learn into practiced discipleship.

The Secure Leader's Leadership

22

Do exactly what you would do if you felt most secure.

—MEISTER ECKHART

I 'll admit, I didn't feel up to the challenge of ministry when God called me to serve Him as a pastor. And with good reason. I really *wasn't* up to it. But like they say, He doesn't call the equipped; He equips the called. And for each of these thirty-plus years since then, I have endeavored to study and grow and become more secure in my leadership role. Truly, it's the only way to fly!

I have touched on some of the following points already, but I give this by way of summary—a capsule version of what God has taught me about the importance of shunning insecurity. By adopting these four principles and improving on them day by day, you will look back a few months or years from now and recognize that God has done something transformational in your life. I promise you, especially on the heels of this first one:

1. *A secure leader does not fear risk.* Too many church leaders do what they're *supposed* to do but never really get out there and do what they *want* to do—just because they're afraid to. As a result, they spend far too much time contemplating the fear of failure instead of the victories and successes they might enjoy if they run a risk and go for it.

Risk and adventure go hand in hand. You don't get one without the other. Yes, there's an edge out there that can scare us nearly to death—and there are some edges we honestly shouldn't tiptoe near—but faith instills within us the capacity to hazard risk. If we don't, we should expect little more than an endless string of humdrum days at the office, not really stirring much . . . nor stirring much of anything worthwhile in those around us.

We could go so far as to say that without risk, leadership doesn't really exist. If your ideas don't involve a measure of danger or unpredictability, then your church or organization really doesn't need you. If the net effect would result in only a minimal change of direction, policy, or service, why even bother? Why go to the trouble? Why do they need you for things they could easily figure out for themselves?

Leadership without risk is like nailing a lid on top of your potential, afraid to trust God for more than you've already got, while watching what you do possess leak out through the bottom or spoil inside the case. One of the main things required of your leadership is to remove anything that forces a ceiling on where your group can go. You may fail at times along the way—no doubt about that—but risk is the only way to adventure. And adventure is the only way to the kind of success that really matters.

Because this point about risk taking is frightening to so many, I feel that I cannot emphasize it enough. If you're a leader who clings to certainty, who obsesses over obstacles, who almost always prefers staying put, I implore you to rethink your position, not only for your own benefit but also for your followers. Perhaps you've inherited a church or other organization that's mired in immobility, paralyzed by fear of change. To quote Mark Twain, "Loyalty to petrified opinion must be broken"—not by force but by leading, by leadership. It is up to you whether or not this enterprise will die on the vine or abound with new growth as God gives you His favor.

Has God placed within you a dream, a vision for what could be if you were unrestrained by risk aversion? Maybe you share the sentiment one of our youth pastors once said to me: "I would hate to die with this dream in my heart." Then don't. Get out there. Dare to do it. Take a risk.

Are you frustrated by the lack of initiative and enthusiasm in your other church leaders? Bold challenges have a way of forcing people off center, stimulating intensity, placing them in a position of dependence on God for His supernatural intervention. Every church I've pastored was in need of some major change. Maybe it's time. Time to try. Time to shake things up. Time to risk.

Is stagnation taking over throughout your congregation? Are all your ideas old and tired? Has excitement waned until it's become the expectation? What's to lose, then, from taking some chances, from breaking new ground, from running a risk?

You will never tap into your full potential as a leader or as an organization if you don't. It's been said that five years from now, we will be the same people we are today except for the books we read, the people we meet, the places we go, and the risks we take. Be secure enough in both God's calling and His equipping to try something you've never tried before but have always wanted to. Win or lose, at least it'll be an adventure!

2. *A secure leader instills capacity for ministry in others.* It goes without saying (or without saying again) that an insecure leader has a hard time promoting anyone but himself. But those who strive to lead with strength and assurance will not only *promote* others, they'll invest in them with purpose, increasing others' potential for success.

Think of the well-known rivalry that King Saul percolated between himself and young David. Had Saul been a secure leader, he not only would have been glad to count someone of David's skill on his side, he would have relished the opportunity to contribute to David's future success. We see just the opposite in Paul who, bearing some of the same rationales for wanting to consolidate power and control within himself, freely built into others' lives. To cite one of numerous examples, Titus 1:4–5 has him writing a young man he had led to the Lord and mentored in the faith, instructing him to "appoint elders in every town." This indeed was "the reason I left you in Crete," Paul said—to expand the base of leadership, to enlarge the potential for ministry, and to involve more people in the work God was doing.

We should be secure enough in ourselves and in the sure plans of God not only to appoint people to leadership but also to be active in helping them excel. Rather than sending people into the fray to fend for themselves, setting people up to fail, we must provide them the preparation and information necessary to help them be their best in God's service.

3. *A secure leader empowers people.* The authoritarian, insecure approach to leadership overlooks the fact that people desire by nature to contribute to a worthy cause. But how can an organization hope to grow if people are not allowed to exercise their spiritual gifts into making a difference? How can you preside over anything of value without the heart and muscle of many others who are eager to contribute to the goal?

The greatest leader of all time, our Lord Jesus Christ, modeled this Himself. He said to His disciples, "I will give you the keys of the kingdom of heaven, and whatever you bind on earth is already bound in heaven, and whatever you loose on earth is already loosed in heaven" (Matt. 16:19). He employed His people in the noble work, giving them large responsibilities to fulfill. We should do the same.

Many of the people who consider joining our church ask me, "Will we be needed there?" They want to be part of what we're doing, not apathetic, uninspired, and uninvolved. Even secular managers are discovering that their workers are most satisfied when they're being stretched and challenged. People have an inborn desire to be motivated to great things. Secure leaders recognize this and delight in empowering them to assist the vision.

4. *A secure leader does not revel in position but in mission.* A lot of people just want the title. Others, however, much prefer knowing that they're doing something significant, contributing to the success of their enterprise. That's what

matters. The goal of leadership is not to gather a bunch of followers, to pile up more people under your name on the organizational chart. The goal of leadership—and the actual result of *secure* leadership—is to reproduce more leaders.

A church should never say, "We want more members so we can get bigger and be noticed. We're after megastatus!" Come on. That kind of attitude can never find satisfaction since it's based on a faulty premise and misses the whole point. Churches grow God's way when people are being discipled into action, raised up to reach their spiritual potential, put into places where God can use them to touch even more lives. Secure leaders couldn't care less what's written on their business card. They just want to know that their passion for God's glory and gospel is being written into people's lives, who are taking it and writing it in their own words into even *more* people's lives.

May God give us secure leaders that see incredible potential in others, passing their legacy on to the generations to follow. May one of those leaders be me. And another be you.

The Leader's Spouse

23

*My most brilliant achievement was my ability to be able
to persuade my wife to marry me.*

—WINSTON CHURCHILL

I'm writing this chapter while vacationing with my wife
in a southwestern town in Mexico. Our two children
and their spouses along with our four grandchildren will
be arriving soon as we prepare to celebrate Thanksgiving
together. But today is a special day all its own.

It's our thirty-eighth wedding anniversary.

So while I believe the truths I'm about to share are helpful reading for any leader and his spouse—advice that can
help each of you be a blessing to the other—I confess I feel
the need to brag on my wife this morning. I cannot imagine
where I'd be without her. Not here. Not pastoring a church.

Not being the president of our denomination. Not writing a book on leadership—or on anything. I'd be lucky to be alive, most likely. I'm serious.

And yet that is the power of the leader's wife—the ability to impact one particular person so dramatically that he is able (by her important presence in his life) to impact many. That has certainly been the case in my experience. I hope and pray it is the case in yours.

But if it's not, I trust this tribute to my wife of thirty-eight years will still inspire you to gather yours close to you, shower her with your affection, and thank her for what she *has* been to you. None of us is perfect. We are all capable—and guilty—of being less than we should be to each other. And yet God can heal and restore even the most lifeless marriage into one that resonates with His blessing. I've seen it happen. I know it can.

Solomon, famous for his wisdom, once wrote, "A man who finds a wife finds a good thing and obtains favor from the LORD" (Prov. 18:22). He also said, "A house and wealth are inherited from fathers, but a sensible wife is from the LORD" (Prov. 19:14). A leader needs a lot of things to help him reach his greatest potential, but none is greater than the person God has placed in his life to complete him and serve at his side. Outside of a personal relationship with the Lord Jesus Himself, the most valuable possession in a leader's heart is his wife. God has designed us that way. And in order for this relationship to be its very best, the following nine attributes must be present.

1. *The leader's spouse believes in him.* I wrote in the chapter on "Leaders Need Respect" how important it is for a man to be respected by his wife. Again, the Bible is very specific

about this. Unlike what some psychologists contend, that man's greatest need is sex, I find no biblical support for this claim. As pleasurable and important as sexual intimacy is within marriage, "the wife is to respect her husband" (Eph. 5:33). That's her ultimate gift and responsibility to him.

My wife, Janet, has certainly made good on this account. When I have not had the capacity to believe in myself, my wife has always been there, believing in me, encouraging me, respecting me. Seeing farther than I could see—seeing *before* I could see—she has not been surprised at the opportunities God has afforded and entrusted to me. She knew from the very beginning that God was up to something special in my life. Even when I was nowhere close to believing it myself, she believed in me. Many times her belief in me was the only reason I could press on. What I saw as surprises, she saw as expectations. Hard as it's been for me to believe, she has believed in me.

2. *The leader's spouse encourages him.* When Janet and I married, she was seventeen, still a junior in high school, yet attending regularly, making straight *A*s, and holding down a job on the side. I was eighteen, a high school dropout with an eleventh grade education, no passion for school, and really a man without peace and with no spiritual direction. All of that changed when Jesus Christ intersected my life. I immediately began to sense that God wanted to use me. But it was the engine of Janet's encouragement that really took this truth from idea to action. She encouraged me to go to night school to earn my GED, persuaded me to pursue a bachelor's degree in religion, took a part-time job (while also tending to our firstborn child), and kept the encouragement coming night and day, week after week.

It made a huge difference in getting me ready for future ministry.

3. *The leader's spouse supports him.* Very soon after beginning my college work at Gardner-Webb, the Lord provided an opportunity for me to pastor a small church in the area. When this position arose, my wife quit her job to have more time available for me. Even though she couldn't read a note of music, she began leading the children's choir, growing it into a marvelous little program. As the church began attracting new families, the inadequacy of our nursery facilities became rather glaring. So she cleaned out a room in the church, decorated it beautifully, and began offering care herself to the small children. She supported me then; she continues to support me till this day. I have never been without her backing and assistance.

4. *The leader's spouse loves him unconditionally.* I've made some bad choices in life, in work, and in ministry. Especially early on, I didn't always use the best judgment in placing people in leadership. I didn't always respond properly when people had a complaint. But when I got home, I could be sure to find someone who loved me, encouraged me, and challenged me to do what was right. Matters I had struggled with all day—and was still unsure about what to do—Janet could often see clearly and quickly. But where she could have berated or belittled me, she loved me instead, even when I was coming up short and needing help. There is no substitute for that kind of real-world, real-time affection.

5. *The leader's spouse completes him.* There is something missing when Janet is not there. We don't function as well apart as we do together. Her presence and perceptiveness

fill in places where my heart is weak and incomplete. She is used of God to meet needs in my life as no one else can.

6. *The leader's spouse knows him.* Some days when I come home from the office, she may simply ask, "How was your day?" I'll say something cryptic and nondescript, like, "It was fine." She'll respond—with nothing more to go on than that tiny bit of information—"What was so bad about it?" She knows me. She knows me all too well. She understands my moods, my voice inflections, my hurts, my sensitivities. She knows exactly how to speak into my life when things seem out of control. A man needs that in his wife.

7. *The leader's spouse trusts him.* Janet knows that for me to follow the dreams God has placed on my life, I need to be out speaking, encouraging others, challenging them, exercising my spiritual gift. This is a cause for sacrifice on her part. It often takes me away from home, leaving her behind to handle the day-to-days. But she trusts me enough to release me to pursue my obedience to God's call. I am forever indebted to her for this kind of love and respect. She makes me want to be excellent in my leadership role, and she makes me want to hurry home to be with her again. It's a beautiful thing.

8. *The leader's spouse doctors him.* I'm not sure about you, but I've heard people say that men are the biggest babies in the world. (Who are they kidding?) OK, so we don't do pain very well and don't make very good patients as a rule. But I know that when I'm sick, my sweet Janet is always right there by my side, taking care of me the same way she might take care of one of our grandchildren (and usually letting people know that I'm much more of a baby than any four- or seven-year-old). Guilty as charged!

9. *The leader's spouse cares for him.* It's not hard to tell if someone really loves you dearly and deeply. I have been blessed for these thirty-eight years with a wife who leaves no question that she does. She truly cares about what I need and graciously provides it without complaint or resentment. I am so grateful for a wife who's gracious and willing to meet me where I am. I hope your testimony is much the same.

It is true that a man who finds a good wife finds a good thing. Janet Lee Allen Hunt is a good thing to me. Every leader needs someone at his side who bears all nine of these qualities. That leader has unbelievable potential and capacity to become everything he desires to be.

Thank you, Janet.

I love you.

Leaders
Serve Others

24

Love cannot remain by itself—it has no meaning.
Love has to be put into action, and that action is service.

—MOTHER TERESA

D r. Bill Early has the kind of medical practice anyone in his profession would envy: a full patient load. Pleasant, satisfied staff. High regard—and high demand—for both his skill and demeanor. He runs out of appointment slots long before he runs out of referrals. His is a thriving, successful office.

Not every doctor has it so good. Not all of Dr. Early's colleagues can attest to running at the same capacity. Surely they're busy doing *something* while they keep you reading magazines in their waiting rooms for so long, but it's not always because they're flooded with patients. Not every doctor exudes the kind of confidence that leads to repeat business.

So among those who know, Dr. Early's practice stands out as one worth emulating. Other doctors often ask him how he does it, what's the secret to his success. As he told me one day recently over lunch, if there is any secret at all, it's as simple as this: he thinks of everyone who comes into his office as a person he can serve. It's a deliberate mind-set, the kind that says, "Every time God sends me a patient, I want to do my absolute best to take care of that person."

Success is not a business plan. But service is. When people know you're there to serve them, they'll come back. They'll tell their friends. They'll still be coming back years and years down the line. The doors are nearly guaranteed to stay open on those enterprises built around serving their customers, their clients—even their church members.

Service stands out.

Harry Bullis, former chairman of the board of General Mills, used to give his salesmen the following advice: "Forget about the sales you hope to make, and concentrate on the service you want to render." When a person's focus is on serving others, he becomes more energized and dynamic.

But most people apparently haven't gotten the memo on this. A substantial percentage of those who call your church their home come to be served, to receive, to take up a space and soak up the special treatment. As a result, not only do these individuals miss out on the purest joy that life has to offer, the church is also stunted in its growth and effectiveness. It takes all of us as leaders—including the leaders we are constantly drawing up from within our congregations—to demonstrate with our lives that service is God's way to greatness.

The cool thing about Christianity and its living expression through the church is that everyone—*everyone!*—has the capacity for greatness by virtue of Christ's saving, sanctifying work in their hearts. It works like this: Jesus said, "Whoever wants to become great among you must be your servant" (Matt. 20:26). The word used here for "servant" is the Greek *doulos* (pronounced, DOO-los), which refers to an underrower, one whose expressed purpose is serving. Jesus ascribed this trait to Himself in Matthew 20:28: "The Son of Man did not come to be served, but to serve, and to give His life—a ransom for many."

My desire in this chapter (as well as the next couple of chapters) is to remind you of what you already know—that life is literally a place of service—and to encourage you to refocus your attention on what makes leadership the noble and God-honoring activity it is.

Speaking of refocusing, one of the greatest threats to your capacity for service is linked to how you respond to failure. I've spent a fair share of this book warning about the dangers of fearing failure. I've reinforced the fact that mess-ups and do-overs are a part of courageous leadership. But if we're not careful, we can find on the other side of failure a leadership path that is consumed with preservation, with rationalizing, with spin and distraction and damage control. We can unwittingly allow our ministry mistakes to multiply on us by letting them subtly turn our focus away from others and onto ourselves.

So although it may seem odd to be connecting the dots this way—between service and failure response—receive the following truths as a means of keeping your servant's mind sharp, even when the strain of leadership is at its toughest:

1. *All leaders fail.* Leaders are not exempt from making mistakes, sometimes big ones. So don't try to hide every failure or pretend they don't exist. If you do, you insult your people's intelligence. Confess it and move on. The Bible says, "Though a righteous man falls seven times, he will get up, but the wicked will stumble into ruin" (Prov. 24:16).

2. *Times of failure reveal a leader's true character.* Whenever I think about the fact that a person's character and tenacity and big-picture perspective are all demonstrated in how he responds to failure, I'm reminded of a principle that Dr. Jerry Falwell taught me years ago. Quoting the truth found in Proverbs 24:10 (NKJV)—"If you faint in the day of adversity, your strength is small"—he went on to say that a man's greatness is determined by how much it takes to discourage him. Leaders have learned that failures will happen in life, but a good leader will not allow it to keep him down or so discourage him that he can't yet make another attempt.

King David certainly made some major mistakes, but when called to account for them—such as when he conducted a census of the people to God's displeasure in 1 Chronicles 21:17, or more famously, when the prophet Nathan confronted David concerning his sin with Bathsheba and against her husband, Uriah—David was honest about it (see 2 Sam. 12). He had made some damaging choices that would continue to affect his life in harmful, hurtful ways. Yet when his guilt became clear to him, his true character was revealed. He was always honest about his shortcomings, owned up to them, and sought to rectify them.

It's been said that it's always too soon to quit, and here's the reason and motivation why: we are servant leaders. God has called us to serve others. We can't allow a little thing (or even a big thing) like failure to divert us from our purpose. We must let times of disappointment with ourselves grow us closer to Christ and make us more diligent to fulfill our priority of servanthood.

3. *Times of failure invite transparency.* True servanthood requires an open, obvious expression of ourselves. We don't help anybody—and don't stay servant leaders very long—by being disingenuous or hiding behind a public face. And few things have the potential for inspiring transparency like admitted failure. Not only does this kind of openness make us more service minded; it also reduces the chances that we'll make some of the same mistakes again. Transparency is essential in a leader. By serving others in this way, you can expect others to be real and genuine with you as well.

4. *Times of failure can foster new responsibility.* A real leader always takes the blame—proactively, voluntarily—for any failure in his organization, not shifting the blame to others. Later there may be an appropriate time for addressing and dealing with specific matters in private, but we must take ownership for that which we lead. People will appreciate this quality in you. Your loyalty in these crisis moments will be remembered many years past, returning to you by way of greater intensity and focus in your followers. This is a pivotal way of serving those who look to you for leadership.

5. *Times of failure present opportunities for significant leadership lessons.* A couple of years ago, it became quite obvious to those of us in leadership at First Baptist Church, Woodstock, that we were not only enduring a season of

plateaued ministry, we were actually declining in growth and effectiveness. I couldn't understand why. It wasn't until, fatigued and frustrated, I took some time away to read, pray, and meditate on the Word that I discovered the reason why. The problem was . . . me. I had been too busy, sidetracked by line items that were not as important as the priorities that had guided my life thus far. I had lost my focus in leading our church. It was during this time of failure and realization that Jesus led me to recommit myself to Him and to the task of servant leadership. This became for me a time of serving our church and our leaders by teaching them what God had done in correcting my steps. It became a time, thanks to my election as president of the Southern Baptist Convention, to vocalize these lessons from a larger platform to churches throughout the nation. Failure had taught me some things. It made me a better servant.

None of us like to admit fault and misdirection. We much prefer to be recognized for our foresight and follow-through, our flawless expertise. But the admission of failure often opens the most effective door to strong leadership, the door that is later recognized as a turning point in our ministries. Our enemy will use anything he can to keep us from being servanthearted, to keep us from being "great" in the kingdom of heaven.

Never forget what's most important. Never forget that you've been raised to heights of leadership to mine the depths of service.

Leaders Serve *with* Others 25

Good company and good discourse are the very sinews of virtue.

—IZAAK WALTON

People often ask me as a pastor, "How much time should I spend with my staff?" There's not really a measurable, numerical answer to that question, but I can tell you this: the strength of your staff is your relationship with them. I don't really see myself as serving *over* those I lead as much as serving *beside* them. We work together. We're a team. We make a point of connecting with each other, getting to know one another, not being threatened or competitive or at varying purposes.

I have learned and observed that if a leader doesn't relate well with his staff, he won't be able to relate well with his people. We need to be extremely comfortable together. We need to enjoy times around the lunch table, in each other's homes, on the golf course, as well as in the office. Our relationship will bear bountiful fruit in our shared ministry, enabling us to unite more effectively—and joyfully—in serving Christ and serving others.

If you're in agreement with me on this, I'd expect you might like to call one of your staff members or key laypeople here in a minute just to speak a word of encouragement, talk through a little matter of ministry, or just see how his or her day's been going. So in the interest of hands-on application, I'm going to toss out five points for you to think about:

1. *Position does not automatically translate to followship.* People may respect your title, but their eagerness to follow you will have a lot less to do with *what* you do than with how you do it. Staying connected with your leadership team earns you the privilege of being followed.

2. *Leadership and relationship go together.* Do not compartmentalize the two, thinking that leadership happens best when you're alone making plans on your laptop. Leaders certainly need time to themselves, and some things must be done in quiet, but the bulk of your leadership is built around times of relating, letting people see who you really are, giving them the opportunity to listen and buy in.

3. *When leaders develop their relationship skills, they help themselves.* I assure you, if you would be more intentional in your relationships, you could afford to be less intentional in your leadership. People follow more naturally those they feel a true connection with. Being relational and compassionate toward your staff will result in greater acceptance of your guidance.

4. *Relationship building must be genuine.* It's not hard to spot a phony, a leader who's only doing this because he read a book that told him to. The best leaders have a genuine adoration for others, a true love and respect for them. They honestly admire the giftedness in the body of Christ, the way their staff and other leaders do what they do. They appreciate other people in a clearly authentic manner. They know they couldn't do this without them. In fact, they wouldn't *want* to do it without them.

5. *People like working in caring places.* If a pastor stays in a church long enough, the people will take on his personality. That can be a scary thought, especially if the leader is not relational. But if he is strong at building relationships, the people around him will share his heart. If you don't like the way your church looks right now, it's possible that it may be a reflection of the one who's leading. Ask God's help in making you even more of a caring person, and you'll find yourself leading a caring church.

When we think about relational leadership and serving with others, the leadership heart of the Lord Jesus Christ springs quickly to mind. Let's see what we can learn from His example in this:

1. *Jesus loved His people.* John 13:1 says, "Before the Passover Festival, Jesus knew that His hour had come to depart from this world to the Father. Having loved His own who were in the world, He loved them to the end." I trust this will one day be said of us, that we loved our people, the ones who served alongside us . . . and that we loved them "to the end."

2. *Jesus put others ahead of His own agenda.* The scene where He washed His disciples' feet is perhaps the most

descriptive portrait of this undeniable truth. When those around Him were becoming worried and confused about all that was taking place and what the future might hold, Jesus laid His own concerns aside to minister to His followers. This should be our objective as well.

3. *Jesus possessed the confidence to serve.* The Bible tells us that Jesus was able to serve the people around Him because He "knew that the Father had given everything into His hands, that He had come from God, and that He was going back to God" (John 13:3). Indeed we have too many insecure leaders, resulting in too many insecure staff members, because the leader isn't convinced that God is sovereignly at work in the leader's heart and ministry.

4. *Jesus initiated service to others.* He didn't have to be asked or prompted. In fact, the disciples should have been washing *His* sacred feet, yet He initiated the ceremony Himself. He led by example. Search high and low in the Scripture, and you'll never find Jesus giving a command or challenge to His people that He had not already obeyed in His own life. He is our model in this, as in all things.

5. *Jesus was not worried about His position.* We're back to the first point made at the top of this chapter, but if even Jesus Himself—the Holy One of glory—didn't allow His dignity to prevent Him from being a true servant, how can we? Are you willing to humble yourself for the good of your followers? Do you consider it a privilege to be serving them and serving *with* them? Don't allow yourself to become position-conscious. It keeps others from wanting to follow.

Last but not least, let the godly truths and advice from Romans 12:9–21 be your counselors as you grow in relationship with your leadership team:

- Avoid hypocrisy.
- Be loyal.
- Give preference to others.
- Be hospitable.
- Return good for evil.
- Identify with others.
- Treat everyone with respect.
- Do everything possible to keep peace.
- Don't be a respecter of persons.
- Remove revenge from your life.

Now get out there and let your staff and key laypeople know how you feel about them. Remind them often of their unique value to the ministry of your church. Really get to know them, and let them get to know you. Embrace the challenges by enhancing your relationships.

Leaders Serve *through* Others

26

*Coming together is a beginning. Keeping together
is progress. Working together is success.*

—HENRY FORD

You don't become a successful leader without realizing
that your value is not based on what *you* can do, but
rather on what you can do through others.

This is just another way to say that leadership is all about
people, about others—not merely doing things *for* people
but *through* them, lighting fires in their hearts and then
creating opportunities for the heat to spread. That's how a
leader begins to really make a difference.

And after all, isn't that the result you truly want from
your leadership efforts? To make a difference? To leave
things better than you found them? To be missed when

you're gone because of all the good that happened while you were here?

In order to be a difference maker, it's imperative that you stay committed to others, never leaving them behind or minimizing their importance. As I've said many times before, the leader has no greater resource than the people he leads. No one can do as much alone as he can through others. Here are four ways to put this truth into practice:

1. *Equip, exhort, encourage.* By way of the words you speak and the knowledge you invest into others, God transports people to the places where they can make the most difference. And by igniting this powder keg of potential with the spark of your ongoing encouragement, the possibility of watching others succeed increases at an exponential rate. This is the joy of leadership, this infusion of forward thrust into others' lives. By equipping, exhorting, and encouraging—as well as exemplifying, modeling the same traits of faith and consistency you desire in your followers—you place your ministry on an upward trajectory that outshoots any possibilities you could accomplish on your own.

2. *Be desperate, determined, directed.* Ask yourself, "Am I *dying* to see a great work for God accomplished through our church and our people?" If not, then there's not really a whole lot of point in getting everybody's hopes up. Being about our Father's business is not something we can play at or pretend about. If His glory and kingdom gain is not what shakes us from sleep each morning, we shouldn't expect it to be a matter of practical importance in those we lead. When the great sixteenth-century reformer John Knox prayed, "Lord, give me Scotland or I die," he sensed the Lord responding, "Die, John Knox, and I will give you Scotland."

This desire for the work of God must be in your gut. People will follow that kind of passion. They'll want to be part of what you're talking about.

3. *Stay involved, invested, intense.* Yes, we're committed to drawing up the potential that God has placed in others, but not so we can turn them loose while we sit back and lose ourselves in distracted priorities or personal projects. You cannot make a difference by proxy. You must be personally involved in what you're asking of others. You must stay available for counsel and corrective adjustments. You must demonstrate what you believe in by *doing* what you believe in. As the one who is setting the tone and casting the vision, you cannot afford to let your intensity be compromised by inattention. You're not just *building* the team, you're *on* the team. Stay suited up. Your followers need to see you keeping yourself in fighting shape.

4. *Be something, going somewhere, with somebody.* Leaders are able to see the possibilities first. That's what makes you a leader. God has given you the capability of seeing first and seeing farther. You may live under the same sky as everyone else, but there are horizons that only you can locate and lock on to. One of your main jobs as a leader is to capture these lofty dreams in words, pictures, and practices that others can grasp and desire. Before the people will go with you, they must have a clear idea of where you're taking them. And where you're taking them needs to be someplace bigger than *you* are, a place that requires everyone to set on the journey together.

This is the distinction in a difference-making mentality. It's not the picture of a leader detached from his people, basking in the privileges of his position. It's not the idea of a leader who can talk a good game from the pulpit but loses his luster when dealing with people one-on-one. It's not a man who's enamored by his Rolodex and allergic to his work gloves. Leaders who can look back on lives of significance are those who are seriously submitted to God's lordship, firmly convinced of their people's value, and devoted to the prospect of working together to achieve everything the Lord has planned for this ministry.

Others. Together. Each of us performing the tasks God has called us to fulfill. This is the secret to great accomplishment, and this should be a chief goal of our leadership. We outperform our individual potentials when each of us is doing our part faithfully and for the Lord's renown. I like the way this anonymous poem says it:

Why Did God Put Me Here?

I don't know how to say it, but somehow it seems
    to me
That maybe we are stationed where God wanted
    us to be;
That little place I'm filling is the reason for my
    birth,
And just to do the work I do, He puts me on this
    earth.

If God had wanted otherwise, I reckon He'd have
    made
Me just a little different, of worse or better grade;
And since God knows and understands all things
    of land and sea,
I fancy that He placed me here just where He
    wanted me.

Sometimes I get to thinking, as my labors I review
That I should like a higher place with greater tasks
    to do;
But I come to the conclusion when envy is stilled
That the post to which God sent me is the post He
    wanted filled.

So I plod along and struggle in the hope when day
    is through
That I'm really necessary to the things God wants
    to do;
And there isn't any service I can give which I should
    scorn,
For it may be just the reason God allowed me to
    be born.

Leadership That Lasts

27

> *If I have seen farther than others, it is because*
> *I was standing on the shoulders of giants.*
>
> —ISAAC NEWTON

Leaders are more noted these days for coming and going than for sticking and lasting, It's rare anymore for a pastor to stay much longer than three years at his current place of ministry.

Three years!

One of my mentors, Dr. Homer Lindsay Jr., who enjoyed a lengthy leadership post at First Baptist Church in Jacksonville, Florida, said that it takes five to six years to really become a pastor to any one group of people. If his math is about right—and I believe it is—the average pastor today will never become the man God has called him to be. That's a staggering thought.

This is not to say that it's absolutely counter to the will of God to ever accept another position or to rise to a new leadership challenge. What's troubling to me is the reason behind many of these moves. Most ministers who pull up stakes to head elsewhere are seeking greener pastures and an escape from their current set of insurmountable problems. Invariably, however, they find themselves in new pastures that are growing less green by the day, surrounded by nothing but a brand-new assortment of insurmountable problems.

The same, only different. That's the sad sum-up of the status quo for way too many leaders today.

Listen, if problems were the reason why a leader should move on, Moses would have never gotten Israel out of Egypt, much less across the Red Sea. Joshua would have never made it any further than Ai. Gideon would have continued working on the threshing floor and never defeated the Midianites. David would have stayed with the sheep and never glorified God by killing Goliath. Daniel would have never risen to godly prominence in the Babylonian empire or experienced God as the lion tamer He is. Jeremiah would have quit prophesying. Peter would have quit preaching and gone back to fishing. Stephen would have been lost to history rather than celebrated as a hero of the early church. Paul would have stuck to tentmaking and never taken a missionary journey. Jesus would have never died on the cross.

Problems are not the problem. The problem in leadership circles today is a lack of perseverance, the kind of gutsy tenacity that battles through what others work around, the dedication that has always been the difference between results and regrets.

We need leaders today who will stick by the stuff. We need leaders with a tough hide and a tender heart. We need leaders who will endure no matter the cost. We need leaders that last.

So I am compelled to (and comfortable about) taking the same tack as the apostle Peter, who said to his readers, "I will always remind you about these things, even though you know them" (2 Pet. 1:12)—these contributing factors to longevity in leadership:

Follow God, not personal agenda. That's why the Lord was specific in admonishing us to preach the Word both in season and out of season, to "persist in it whether convenient or not" (2 Tim. 4:2). As pastor and Bible teacher Stephen Olford used to say, "There is no closed season on preaching." The Bible serves as God's blueprint and agenda for His church. Whenever you doubt your directional sense, break out the compass of His Word. Both He and it can always be trusted—always more than your own ideas.

Do not be consumed by the ways of the world. When Abraham's nephew Lot decided to pitch his tent toward Sodom—toward the prevailing, corrupting culture of his day—he not only moved into the world, the world moved into him. And if we're not careful, the same thing can happen to us. The best way to invite confusion over God's will into your life is to make it share space with a worldly mindset. We do have to live here. We don't have to buy into the program. We can't, in fact, if we want to lead and last.

Be concerned for others' welfare. This could be number one, number ten, number twenty, number anything. Leadership is not about us; it's about Him and it's about them. Never, ever forget that. Be reminded of it anew every day.

Move at the command of God. We should be up every morning reading His Word and listening for His mandates. And when He speaks, we must move. When we move, we have the privilege of joining Him in seeing the world changed.

Take others with you. With the exception of two dear saints—Ms. Edna Whitmire and Jim Hamby, both of whom are with the Lord—the entire committee who brought me to First Baptist Church in Woodstock, Georgia, is still here, still committed to Jesus, still following my leadership as their pastor. What greater joy than to walk for so long with such faithful believers! I have put my confidence in them, just as they have put their trust in me. We do what we do together. That's how leaders last.

Spot pitfalls. Author and humorist Arnold H. Glasow said, "One of the tests of leadership is to recognize a problem before it becomes an emergency." The path ahead is littered with snares and traps and all kinds of ambushes. Leaders must be on the watch for these, maneuvering around them with care, protecting not only the mission but also the people involved.

Be decisive. M. Scott Peck said, "The best decision makers are those who are willing to suffer the most *over* their decisions but still retain their ability to be decisive." There comes a time when we must stop analyzing and start acting. People look to you for that. It gives them confidence. When they know you are seeking to hear from your heavenly Father and to stand with His Word in both your hand and your heart, they will follow as you lead. Frequent indecisiveness is a good way to lose followers and a bad way to hope for long ministry. When God initiates something in your heart, bring it before your people and take them on the journey with you. Don't hesitate.

Set people in the right direction. It's a tall order, I know, but it's a primary task of leadership. We must lead with the end in mind. We must know where we're headed and where we're taking our people. And we can only know this by spending quality time with the Lord, perceiving His heart, and then proceeding with boldness, speaking with confidence and clarity in regard to what He has shown us.

Don't live in the past. Thank God for what you have seen thus far in your work, through your ministries, and as a result of your leadership. But believe each morning that the best is yet to be, and lead the people to a bright tomorrow. Otherwise, your leaders will not follow them there.

Don't be satisfied with the status quo. This is not an excuse for comparing ourselves with others. Nothing ever comes of that except frustration and crossed signals. But if our leadership is to last, we must compare our present situation with where we've been, making sure that we're achieving the God-given potential of this moment in time. The standard must be raised and advanced or we will find ourselves slipping backward, becoming increasingly ineffective and fruitless in our efforts.

Maintain a big vision. "Without revelation," the Scripture says in Proverbs 29:18, "people run wild, but one who keeps the law will be happy." I believe God restrains His people from confusion, from boredom, and from a slippage in their moral integrity and intensity when their leaders have a vision, a word from the Lord. Leaders that last give their people something real—and really big—to aspire to. Leaders who don't are too easy to ignore.

Don't be afraid of God's will. I confess to times when I've sensed God's stirring in my heart concerning something He was leading me to do, but I've balked at it. Too bold. Too risky. Too far out of my comfort zone. I wonder what I've missed as a result? Surely the reward would have been worth the risk. We as leaders cannot afford to be afraid of what God is showing us through His Word, through prayer, through either our private times of devotion or a timely comment instigated by the Holy Spirit. It's not our job to make sense of what God is saying but merely to obey when He confirms it. As nineteenth-century businessman and philanthropist George Peabody said, "Our task is not to bring order out of chaos but to get work done in the midst of chaos"—even if what seems chaotic and out of kilter is actually a clear command from the Lord.

Trust God. Charles Spurgeon said, "God has promised to keep His people, and He will keep His promise." Yes, God can be trusted. Jesus never fails. Great leaders go to the bank on that.

Never accept second best. We must not be satisfied with small dreams and mediocre ministries. If you're feeling rigidly stuck in a place of plateaued effectiveness, there's bound to be an answer, an alternative to get you moving forward and upward again. It's not hard to shy away from what's required. The bar can feel as though it's set too high. The standard can seem too demanding. We may not be willing to pay the price. But second best is no place to lay down your leadership. Place yourself on the altar, reminding yourself that God has permission to make the proper repairs in you.

And as He does, lead on with honesty, transparency, and unwavering trust.

I'm convinced in my heart that you and many others who are reading these words are in need of hearing this today, amid your specific set of circumstances. So I say it as clearly and succinctly as I know how. Hang in there! Stay focused. Keep believing. Don't give up. Your best days are still ahead, probably from right here at this particular outpost of God's kingdom. Want it. Seek it. Do it.

"By your endurance gain your lives" (Luke 21:19).

Leaders Moving Off the Plateau

28

The great thing in the world is not so much where we stand,
as in what direction we are moving.

—OLIVER WENDELL HOLMES

Assuming that the numbers are giving us an accurate readout, it is estimated that 85 to 90 percent of all Southern Baptist churches in America are either plateaued or in a state of decline. Only 15 percent—or less—are actually growing.

I know a little bit about plateaued churches. As I shared in a previous chapter, our church in the greater Atlanta area began to plateau in the last couple of years, then began to enter a period of decline. It shook our leadership team up. It shook *me* up. I am aware that many pastors serve churches located in small, fairly confined communities. Ours is not.

How could this be happening at a church with so much exposure and forward momentum, with so many people around us who are lost and in need of a Savior?

I learned some things as a leader while going through this downward cycle in our church's development. I learned from the dictionary that a plateau is a level expanse of elevated land. It doesn't have to be a low-lying area. Churches can plateau as easily at a thousand members as they can at a hundred. I also learned some things about the two key words that kept cropping up as we thought about and analyzed what was happening. *Barrier* is a structure that is built in order to prohibit or obstruct passage, something that hinders or restricts. *Growth* means an increase in size or amount.

Plateau. Barriers. Growth. These were the words that haunted and taunted us as we grappled with the situation before us, as we tried to seek God's path for our future, as we prayed about what it would take to dislodge our ministry from the doldrums and see it start ascending again. One breakthrough came for me when I noticed that each of these words has a common thread: they're all nouns. They fall into that grouping of words that identify a person, place, or thing. What we needed was to get our focus out of the noun domain and into the action category. We needed to be guided by verbs, not labels. We needed to concentrate on movement, not subject headings.

Our new word was . . . *grow!*

The noun *growth* is expressed in principle and status. The verbs *grow* and *growing* are expressed in practice and solutions. If we are to experience growth, we must first be caught in the act of growing.

God expects us to grow. Jesus said to His followers,

"I will build My church" (Matt. 16:18). He has a purpose in mind and an action plan for accomplishing it. He instructed us by way of parable to "go out into the highways and lanes and make them come in, so that my house may be filled" (Luke 14:23). He characterized His life as being like a seed that is placed into the ground to die, but in dying "it produces a large crop" (John 12:24). The church, like the individual Christian, is designed to grow. No doubt about it.

Therefore, certain principles exist in helping us turn this realization into reality. Here are a few that I have discovered:

Growing is a process, not an event. At our church, for example, we don't fund-raise for new buildings through a dedicated season of taking pledges and receiving collections. We don't throw a building fund *event;* we maintain a building people *process.* It's something we're constantly doing.

We view the raising of dollars not as a construction investment but as an ongoing opportunity for the Lord to raise spiritual children. We may use an event as part *of* this process, but not as a stand-alone initiative apart *from* the process. We're building people, not buildings. And we're growing as we go, not stopping and starting every time we need to start raising money again. Look at your church's growth as a long-term continuum, overarching the activities that go on beneath the banner of growing.

Growing is an attitude, not an ability. Like I said, I fully understand that many churches are not located in the midst of spiraling civic growth patterns and the sprawl of new home construction. Your church may not be on the traveling path of many new people moving into your area. But although exceptions to the growing rule do exist, there are probably far more unsaved, unchurched people in these communities than those who gather for worship on a given Sunday. The ability to grow is there. But is there an attitude of growing to go with it?

God doesn't love some churches more than others. He doesn't favor one over another, infusing it with growth while the other nine out of ten churches struggle to maintain. The difference is often attitude. Enthusiasm. Belief. Faith. Energy. Desire. That whatever-it-takes mentality. It's not your own human ingenuity or smarts that will enable you to reach your area for Christ as much as it's your attitude— your absolute assurance that God is as engaged and enthused about your church as any other. He will bless those who are genuinely seeking Him and deliberately seeking others.

Growing is stimulated by dissatisfaction. Have you already done everything great you want to do for God in your lifetime? Has He already accomplished the greatest work possible in you? Has your church, ministry, or organization maxed out its potential? Could it not be any better or more effective—could it not grow any bigger and stronger—than it already is?

The leaders who move their people off the plateau are those who know they're involved in a great work, but who also know that it could be even greater. I think of Nehemiah, urged to set aside what he was doing on the wall rebuilding project, shooing away all detractors and distraction by declaring, "I am doing a great work and cannot come down" (Neh. 6:3). Deep within my heart is a desire to do a great, great work for God—some courageous exploit that will bring Him exalted honor and glory while also expanding His kingdom and blessing His people. I'm convinced we haven't done our best work yet. I'm convinced we must keep growing.

Growing is facilitated by vision. There are things you see that your followers may not. You see the lostness in your community—the hopelessness, the spiritual searching, the rampant regret and fatigue. You see physical hurt and need. You see the lack of purpose that both parades itself in the guise of success and degrades itself in lives of depression and despair. You see the harvest. You see the workers. You see what could be if God's people were engaged in God's business.

But actually doing something about what you see—actually growing in your reach and ministry impact—depends on how well you help your people see these things as well. It also depends on how well the people on the outside see you and your church. What are you doing to help them know that you genuinely care, that your doors are wide open, that they are welcome to come experience life among you and be changed by the power of Jesus Christ? Vision is key when it comes to growing.

It's not hard to see that these principles involve real change, even among those churches and groups that are succeeding in many areas. The path off the plateau is a path in every regard—not a place to stay put, not a one-time leap to another position. It's a process. It means movement. It's one foot in front of the other, not hopping all over the place but sticking to the direction where God is leading.

It's remembering that sentences without verbs—just like churches without good leadership—aren't going anywhere.

Putting Growth into Practice

29

He who moves not forward, goes backward.

—JOHANN WOLFGANG VON GOETHE

S ome say that a church can get too big. To which I respond, "Too big for what?" Too big to reach the lost? Too big to minister to hurting people? Too big to be engaged in world-wide missions? Compare the common rationales for staying small—being able to know everybody, maintaining one worship service and Sunday school—and see if those sound like the kind of noble goals that befit the church of the living God.

I like the way former LifeWay consultant Eugene Skelton put it in his essay entitled "Pray for a Big Church":

> If there are people who want to attend because of its program, spirit, fellowship, Bible teaching,

and preaching, are the members to say, "We do not have room for your family; we are already too big"? When the crowds grew too large for Jesus to talk to a few at a time, did He send them away with instructions to come back in smaller groups? Did He not improvise? Did He not use His imagination? Did He not get into a boat and push out from the shore so He could stand and preach where a greater number of people could see and hear Him? Did Jesus change the usual methods so He could reach more people? Did He alter customary practices to share the gospel with larger crowds? If so, then what does this mean for us as a church?

When the house in which Jesus preached became overcrowded, did He tell the people outside that there was no more room for them? Or did He stand there approvingly while men literally tore the roof off to get someone in? Did Simon Peter tell the three thousand converts at Pentecost that twenty-five hundred of them would have to go home because the church specialists said that five hundred members was the optimal size for a church?

Is small somewhat more spiritual than big? How can small be more spiritual than big when often a church is small because of its indifference to the lost, because of its lack of commitment to missions and evangelism. If a church is small because its people do not visit or pray, if a church is small because it does not baptize many people, how can such a group be considered more spiritual than a church that is large because it *does* believe and practice these things?

This thinking may run counter to some of the arguments you've heard and accepted over the years. It may sound arrogant and showy, as though I'm endorsing the accumulation of numbers for numbers' sake. But I ask you to bring these matters before the Lord in honest prayer to see if you are perhaps defending a leadership model that's more comfortable for *you* but not necessarily in keeping with His plans for your church. Growing means that the reach of the gospel is expanding in your neighborhood and community. It means that more people are receiving Christ, and more people who have not taken their faith seriously are joining a fellowship of faith where God can fold them into His greater purpose for their lives. How can that be a bad thing? Aren't growing pains worth the upside of seeing people obedient to the Father and aligning themselves with His will?

I encourage you to concentrate on the following practices that are essential to a growing church, as well as a growing Christian:

Preach and teach the Bible as the Word of God. During the days of the prophets, the people would often assemble for worship, standing before the man of God and asking the question, "Is there a word from the Lord?" It's what we're all still hungry for today. Spiritual growth is impossible apart from a steady diet of the Bible, the Word of God. This is why church growth begins in the pulpit. When a pastor is consumed with instilling God's truth in the lives of his hearers, when he is totally convinced that this eternal Word remains the message of the hour, followers of Christ will be inspired to obey. Those without Christ will be overtaken by His Spirit. The Scriptures are always central to a growing church—a church that's growing the way God desires.

Create an atmosphere of celebration. If there's any place that should be hopeful, alive, and filled with joy, it ought to be the church of the Lord Jesus. Christ lives within us, and His life should shine forth as we bring life to our fellowships. We ought to be fired up to preach, excited to share what God has shown us in our week's study. We should engage ourselves in lively worship befitting the recipient of our praise—not necessarily in the songs we sing but in how we sing them. And when we step from behind our pulpits to walk out our message in real life, we should do so with energy and authenticity. Being a leader in God's church ought to get our juices flowing! For while there's definitely a place for reflection and contemplation in worship and in Christian practice, I see no reason for the quietness of boredom and apathy. There's nothing dull about our Lord Jesus. There should be nothing dull about our worship and our declaration of His truth.

The pastor must be real and relational. People do not want a phony for a pastor, nor do they want a pastor they can't touch or talk to. A shepherd should be—and should *want* to be—with his sheep. I think of this in the context of my own typical Sunday. I get up very early to be with the Lord and to pray through my message. But the work of getting it pulled together has already been done. Sunday is for being with the people. So I arrive at church early, wanting to see as many people as I can. I spend prayer time with the deacons. I go to Sunday school. I continue to greet and visit and look for opportunities to interact all morning. Then normally after worship, my wife and I invite a family out to lunch, perhaps someone who's new to the church or a family that's asked to spend time with us. After a few hours of rest, we return for the evening service, usually going out again afterward to continue the day's fellowship, exercising our spiritual gift for "hanging out." Sunday is my best chance to be with my people. They're here and available, not like other days of the week. And I want to milk this time for all it's worth. Leaders of growing churches look for every chance to be approachable.

Implement some kind of witnessing training. Some churches grow merely by receiving the castoffs from other churches. Some grow because their neighborhood is growing, with new residents (and old Christians) moving in all the time. But the churches that are most alive and infused with the most joy are those that are seeing people swept from the kingdom of darkness right under their noses, where the congregation can see and smell and taste the difference Jesus makes in a person's life. Growing churches are visiting churches, filled with people who are actively engaging the community, inviting family and friends, declaring the good news of Jesus with their work associates and recreational acquaintances. So feel responsible for equipping them with the tools they need to present God's Word to others. Make sharing Christ the expectation, not the exception. The Spirit of God will honor this kind of preparation by instigating encounters where your people can engage their world with the gospel. Guaranteed!

Develop strong Bible study. Just where we began, we're back around to the Word—not just spoken in the corporate gathering of the worship service but fleshed out face-to-face in the context of small groups and Bible study classes. This is where churches grow. It's been said that if a person or family hasn't been welcomed into some small, more personal setting within a few months of their arrival, they will slip quietly out the back door and perhaps be lost to you forever. Bible study serves as an unrivaled arena for ministering to hurting people, not only by listening and responding to their visible needs but by wrapping their lives in the purpose, blessing, and promise of God's principles. These are the people who represent your church's growth—not numbers on a spreadsheet but real families being touched by God's grace and love. What starts in the Word flows on through changed lives. Then *they* become the servants and givers and workers and witnesses, extending God's message to others, ever growing.

Anything wrong with growing this way? Anything unsavory about seeing God change a life, restore a relationship, or set a new course for a family and their legacy? If that's what growing means, what man of God wouldn't sacrifice the safety of smallness for the possibilities of their church's full potential?

Inspiring Others to Grow

30

Without continual growth and progress, such words as improvement, achievement, and success have no meaning.

—BENJAMIN FRANKLIN

O f all the principles and practical strategies for church growth, none can truly be called effective unless they cash out into real life change for people, for individuals—the ones who are coming and growing along with you. Great churches are not built on programs and projects but on people being transformed by the grace and resurrection power of the Lord Jesus Christ, people who are not just members of His church but disciples in His service. Numerical growth that happens any other way is not even worth the calculator batteries it takes to add it up.

It's as simple as this: God doesn't just expect *churches*

to grow; He expects individual Christians to grow. And as a result, the church begins to grow in all the right ways.

Still, you can't force a person to seek and desire growth in the Christian life. Everyone must ultimately take responsibility for his or her own relationship with God. But you as a leader can be an initiator. You can set the standard and model the example. You can foster an environment where growth is expected and put into practice, where equipping and encouragement is constantly available, where people who are serious about following Christ have any number of ways to live it out in service to others.

It starts with *believing* in people, not letting them be satisfied with lives of spiritual stagnation. It starts with declaring what the Bible calls "the beauty of holiness" (Ps. 29:2 NKJV), the manifold blessings God has chosen to shower on those who are faithful and obedient. It starts with investing yourself in their lives, praying that God would give you great patience with them, taking a tough stand on doctrine but dealing tenderly with their hearts. You'd perhaps be surprised how erring on the side of grace with others will lead not to apathy and permissiveness but rather to a zeal on their part for returning to the Lord.

In sharing just a few things that you want to be sure to inspire in your people, I must first challenge you with this: if you want *others* to grow, *you* need to grow. I'm sure I've said it before—I'm sure I'll say it again—but your example is a lot more inspiring than your exhortation, no matter how eloquent and articulate you may be in presenting it. The power of persuasion is not a trick of the tongue. You can never expect others to be more serious than you are about submitting to Christ and letting Him grow you from the inside out. There's no end to what can be learned from a life that's lived well for the Lord Jesus. So as you push yourself to grow and develop, let your experience with Him lead you to naturally encourage the following three growth patterns in your people:

1. *Teach them to have a quiet time.* You know very well, of course, that few things are more essential to Christian growth than intentionally setting aside some time each day to be with the Lord—unhurried, undistracted, uninterrupted. Infuse into your followers a deep and precious love for the Word of God. Provide them with ways to guide them as they study it. Encourage them to memorize particular verses and passages, allowing their quiet moments with God to continue feeding them truth throughout the day. Teach them how to pray and interact with Him on the most personal, most intimate level. And continually strengthen them to stand up to any and every temptation that would lead them away from their private times of devotion. (Don't we all know how often these arise!) Remind them often of the vital importance that's wrapped up in this one activity, this one particular discipline. You will see the change in your people and in your church.

2. *Teach them to be givers.* The more jaded and skeptical among us would call this self-serving. How convenient, they say, for a leader to cloak in spirituality something that pays his salary and funds his ambitions. But have you ever met a truly giving person—whether of meager or wealthy means—who wasn't one of the happiest, most contented, most authentic people you've ever known? Lead the way in this by being generous with your *own* time and money. Open your heart and home and share freely of the resources God has

entrusted to you. Help your people discover for themselves the time-honored truth that "you can't outgive God." It's not about the church always asking them for money; it's about God promising them eternal, kingdom joy on this side of heaven. Lead your followers to grow in this area, not only for everyone else's good but for *their* good as well.

3. *Teach them to be soul winners.* Many, many people withdraw from ever attempting to witness to others about their faith in Christ. Few of them realize, however, that by comforting their fears and reservations, they're only adding the nagging *dis*comfort of guilt, shame, and spiritual staleness to their lives. I'm convinced that there is nothing more effective at skimming the sluggishness off a Christian's spiritual windshield than the pure joy of watching Christ's salvation break out on a needy sinner, a friend, a family member, or a work associate. We've made this too hard. We've built personal witnessing into a monster that no one wants to tangle with. And therefore, Satan wins his daily little victories while many of us on the ultimate winning side stumble along in momentary defeat. This needs to change in a big, big way. Give your people one of their best opportunities to grow in grace: teach and train them to share *God's* grace regularly and intentionally with others.

There are so many other offshoots of these three main objectives—streams and branches that provide people inroads to growth and outlets for service. Things like Bible study classes and small groups. Areas of ministry within the church and community. Exposure and involvement in world missions. As individuals avail themselves of these opportunities, being obedient to what God has called them to do, the church grows as a whole while they grow themselves.

Churches lift off the plateau as its members spread their wings to fly.

One of your main jobs as a leader is to not let church become a business-as-usual undertaking, nor to let your members' experience of Christianity become a Sunday morning anomaly in an otherwise worldly lifestyle. Don't let them off that easily! Point them higher. Make them hungrier. Offer them something eternal and blessed to show for the hours they spend and the lives they lead. What a difference it will make in the lives of your people when they know what God desires for them—when they know that you see growth in their present and future, regardless of their past.

Help them grow, even as *you* continue growing.

Leadership Principles Worth Remembering 31

Important principles may and must be inflexible.

—ABRAHAM LINCOLN

A ll of us have had people in our lives who said things we'll never forget. Some of these statements may have been very negative or hurtful. Others contain a nugget of bad advice, a bit of foolishness we were taught and perhaps followed without knowing any better. Others bring to mind someone's premature opinion of us, one that can still discourage us at the thought. Even this many years later, we can find ourselves expending new energy to overcome the damage it caused or to prove them wrong.

But thank God, not all of these memorable lines from the past are obstacles we've had to work around or rise above. I'm glad our memory banks also contain withdrawals that pick us up and move us forward, statements that set a strong compass direction and keep us magnetically locked to God's unwavering truth.

I spent a little time recalling some of my favorites lately, the ones that have often come back to me over the years when I had a decision to make or felt myself sliding off center. These are only a sampling. I could think of many more. But I encourage you to learn from these as well . . . and to add to them the quality one-liners from your own past as the Lord stirs them to memory:

1. *"Beware the mystery of iniquity."* Manley Beasley, a prominent Southern Baptist evangelist who died in 1990 at only fifty-eight years of age, spoke these words to me when I was just a twenty-something pastor. He said, "Johnny, Satan has a counterfeit for every one of God's promises. The difference is, Satan doesn't deliver on his promises." Whenever my mind has been lured away from godliness by the desirable unknowns of sin, this statement has been a wonderful word of caution and correction for me. Our enemy's mysteries are nothing but lies and destructive distortions, no matter what kind of fancy clothes he dresses them up in. "Take delight in the Lord," Psalm 37:4 says, "and He will give you your heart's desires." What God's promises may lack in mystery, they more than make up for in happy endings.

2. *"As you grow older, simplify and focus."* I've determined that despite evidence to the contrary, life is not as complicated as we've made it out to be. Marriage, pastoring, Christian living—yes, there are uneven places to watch for and potholes to avoid. But it's nothing that a return to the basics can't fix, and nothing that a narrowing of our focus can't help us recapture. Dr. Adrian Rogers shared this bit

of sage advice with me, and I have found it to be increasingly true as I go along. By keeping our eyes on what is most important, we find ourselves more consistently heading in the right direction. It's really pretty simple.

3. *"Make sure Jesus is on the road before you go down it."* Someone has said that we're all just one decision away from doing something stupid. But as teacher and pastor Ron Dunn once told me, we can keep our distance from stupidity if we'll just keep from making a move until we've heard from the Lord. I've certainly made my share of bad decisions—ones I'm grateful to say are behind me. I'm sure I'll make some more before I'm through. But I try hard to maintain a prayer life that keeps me open to God's Word and sensitive to His Spirit. As He leads me and as I stay willing to follow, I know that He will guide me in the direction of His will. We have His Word on that.

4. *"You'll never miss anything you give away."* In an earlier chapter I introduced you to one of the great influencers in my life, a beloved layman named Otis Scruggs. I will be indebted to him until the day I die for the care and blessing he and his wife, Viola, heaped upon my family and me at the first church I pastored. He said these words to me while in a men's store purchasing a suit for me. His smile and lifestyle were the clear evidence that he had found these words to be abundantly true. I'll never forget rushing to his bedside in Shelby, North Carolina, where he had slipped into a coma and was hours away from death. As I knelt down close to this dear man of God, thanking him for believing in me and encouraging me to be my best for Jesus, his eyes suddenly opened. Recognition formed across his face. He made a motion as if reaching for his back pocket, the way he'd done

so many times before to slide some spending money into my hand. Generosity had become such a reflex action for him, he was still trying to give—even on his deathbed, even in that little backless hospital gown he was wearing. Amazing! I've often thought about financial investments of mine that went sour, about money I basically wasted and never knew exactly where it went. I've missed every single dollar that I lost or spent unwisely. But Otis was right, "You'll never miss anything you give away."

5. *"Son, I won't be here forever."* It was Sunday afternoon. I'd been making a hospital visit and was on my way to church for a deacon's meeting. As I pulled up to an intersection, I glanced at my watch. If I took a left, I could be at the church in about five minutes. If I took a right, I'd be only a mile from my mother's home. I'd noticed she wasn't at church that morning. *Might be a good idea to go check up on her,* I remember thinking. But in one of the worst, most regrettable snap decisions of my life, I opted for my scheduled agenda. I figured she was probably fine. Little did I know that I'd never see her again on this earth. Sometime the next morning I received a phone call from my uncle, telling me that my mother had collapsed in her home and was found unconscious. Mom was gone. And I had missed my last chance to see her. My, how my five siblings and I had depended on her over the years. The jobs she worked and the price she paid to keep us cared for as a single mother were beyond description, beyond belief. She had told me before that she wouldn't be here forever. But I had never wanted to believe it. Looking back on it now, I see that she was teaching me a valuable lesson about not taking others for granted, especially those who are closest to us and the

easiest to overlook. Bessie Mae Hunt was a dear one. I'm glad I'll have forever to let her know.

6. *"It takes six years to become a pastor."* I've already shared these words of Dr. Homer Lindsay Jr., the late pastor of First Baptist Church in Jacksonville, Florida. I repeat them here because it's a lesson lost on too many of today's young (and even not-so-young) leaders. It's a message well worth repeating and remembering. They can put your name above the "pastor" slot on the church sign, they can tack "pastor" to your office door, they can even call you "pastor" when they shake your hand in the hallway. But it takes time before people really know if you have a shepherd's heart, if you'll be there when they need you, if you'll stay accessible to this particular flock that Jesus shed His blood for. I've taken this statement to heart and have passed it on to thousands of other pastors. I've come to believe that if a man is going to be used by God to do a great work in his city or community, it will take many things, but among them must be longevity. It takes time to truly become a pastor.

7. *"First, be real. Second, be anointed."* Adrian Rogers had been around the block once or twice, eliminating a lot of nonessentials from his ministry portfolio, when God helped him boil his priorities down to these important two. Sure enough, nothing is more important in the life of a leader than being genuine. There are a lot of things that you and I can never be, but there's one thing we *all* can be—ourselves. And next in line is the second one: being anointed, experiencing the hand and touch of God on our work and witness. This requires a deep spirit of humility, a true desire for Christ to be exalted through everything we do. Dr. Rogers used to say, "Anointing is God's special touch for

the specific task He has called you to do." We are not real leaders without it. We are only as strong as we allow Him to be in us.

8. *"You can't coast for even one day."* Dr. Paige Patterson was president of Southeastern Baptist Theological Seminary when he spoke these words to me in his office one day. He said, "Johnny, the Christian life is like riding a bike. If you stop, you have a tendency to fall over." How true! We can let God work in our life for years and years, even bringing us to a place of name recognition in the body of Christ, only to see our ministry come crumbling down around us by one foolish decision. It's easy to take our eyes off the road, thinking we can handle things just fine without Him for a while. But each day is a new opportunity—not only for advancement but also for failure. Keep your head in the game and your heart in His hand.

9. *"Finish well."* Of all the things I've heard Dr. Billy Graham say, this is the one that really registers with me. And, my, how he has exemplified it with his own life. We'll not really be remembered for how we started or even how we've done along the way. People will most remember how we finished up—whether poorly or strongly. It pays to enter each day with the end goal in mind, letting it be our passion and purpose, our singular pursuit. We've been placed here to do *all* that God planned for us to do, not just the part we've accomplished up to now. Make plans today to finish well.

10. *"If you know what you have and you like it, be reluctant to leave it."* Among my worst nightmares—and I've had it more than once—is dreaming that I've left First Baptist of Woodstock to pastor another church, only to be miserable

for the rest of my life. I can say with all sincerity that when I stand before these dear people on Sundays, ask them to open God's Word, and wait for the pages to stop shuffling as they flip through their Bibles for the right passage, I often think—and sometimes say to them—"I'd rather be here and be your pastor than be anywhere else in the world." I hope you can say that about your current place of service. But if not, I caution you with this: don't be too quick to trade what you have for what you think you want. Things aren't perfect at our church. I've had opportunities to go elsewhere. But I've never been able to get these words of Homer Lindsay's out of my head. They bring me back to reality. They keep me grounded and content. They help me blow away the smoke of abstract dreams and clear my head to see what God is doing—and may still do—right here at my feet. These words are not a call to shut your ears to God's leading, but rather a warning not to trust anyone else's word but His—not even your own. Appreciate what you have and where you are. It's not hard at all to find a place that can make this one look a whole lot better than it does right now.

11. *"Stay close and clean."* In my early days in ministry, pastors younger than myself would often come to me and ask something like, "What's the single most important advice you could pass on to me?" I'd hate to hear some of the things I chose to say in response. But if they were to call me up today, I know exactly what I'd tell them: "Stay close and clean." Every morning with few exceptions, after I've gotten up, washed my face, brushed my teeth, and started the coffee, I walk to a special place in my house that's set aside for being with the Lord. I sit down, I open my Bible, and I start my day in the pure and holy presence of God.

Every morning. I need to be that close. I need the reminder of who He is. I need to refresh my unreliable emotions with His never-ending truth. I need to retrain any wayward logic with His ageless plans and purposes. I often pray in times like these, as I ask the Lord to search me and reveal any sinfulness in my heart, that if He—being omniscient, fully knowing my future—can see a day when I would do anything to bring reproach on His name, His church, or my precious wife, that He would call me home prematurely instead. I desperately want to be in His will, to be passionately attuned to His Spirit, to be about my Father's business. To be close and clean.

The people who first spoke these eleven statements to me would likely never have dreamed the impact their words were having. But each of these principles landed with their full weight in my heart, and they have continued to grow deep roots throughout my lifetime. Take any of these that hit you with that kind of force and welcome them into your spirit. Take the ones you've heard along your own journey, as well, and keep them close to your heart and ready on your tongue—because others are traveling behind you. And they need what you have to share. Good leadership principles are not just for remembering. They're for repackaging and recycling.

The Leader's Assistant

32

Build for your team a feeling of oneness, of dependence on one another, and of strength to be derived by unity.

—VINCE LOMBARDI

It feels appropriate, in discussing what to look for and encourage in an assistant, to begin with this quote from a legendary football coach. That's because administrative assistants—or administrative professionals as they may be called—are the most valuable players in our churches. They are the offensive linemen who protect the quarterback. They're the receivers who catch everything the quarterback throws at them. The running backs who carry the ball when it's handed to them. The defensive linemen who tackle the difficult tasks. The linebackers who handle disgruntled church members. The assistant coaches who implement the game plan. They're even the water boys who come along with a fresh cup of coffee at just the right time. What would we do without them?

I've been blessed by God to have a personal assistant, Mrs. Ruth Blakney—Miss Ruth, as we call her—who has served my office for the last twenty years. She carries herself so capably, exuding one of the most endearing Southern personalities a person could possibly possess, as well as a tender heart for the Lord and a genuine love for His people. She fulfills every one of the qualities outlined in this chapter. In fact, my ability even to write on this subject is based primarily on my many years of watching her exemplify excellence in her work and integrity in her life. What a gift from God she is, has been, and continues to be, not only to me but to so many others.

Why don't you take a minute today to give a great big shout-out to your assistant in some way?

A leader's work and ministry is hugely dependent on his or her ability to involve and utilize an assistant in helping him carry out his ministry. Choosing not to maximize her many gifts and abilities—for whatever reason, be it your insecurity or distrust or any number of contributing causes—is like the one-talent man from Jesus' parable who refused to make use of what was available to him. To do so is poor stewardship not only of your own time but also of hers. She has been employed to assist you in accomplishing the objectives of your calling and ministry. Do not—*do not!*—take from her the hard-fought joy of serving the Lord alongside you.

Truly, the personal assistant to the pastor is a ministry position, just like any other staff member. Encourage her to see her work in this light—vital to the church, instrumental in people's lives, a pleasing offering to the Lord Himself. Never allow her work to be viewed as lowly and unimportant, as menial and second-class. She embodies the kingdom principle of Jesus that states, "Whoever wants to become great among you must be your servant" (Matt. 20:26).

So as you go about hiring a person to fill this role, or as you're leading the one who currently occupies it, keep the following qualities in mind. Even if you lead in the business or corporate arena rather than a church context, these observations should still have a bit of carryover into the type of work you do. Not all of them will line up quite as evenly, perhaps, but look for the ones that will be of help to you in assessing talent and keeping your team strong and intact, ready for anything. I share the following in no certain order of importance:

1. *Positive attitude.* Contrary to what some would believe, working in a church setting is not the equivalent of heaven on earth but a daily mixture of equal parts: sweetness and light. Many problems arise. Complaints come walking through the door or blaring over the telephone. Misunderstandings can often abound. But assistants have the potential of setting the entire atmosphere for the office. Nothing is more depressing than dealing with a negative person. But those who approach the challenges of the day with a positive, healthy spirit can keep an eternal perspective humming along with the office equipment, helping you whistle your way over every bump in the road.

2. *High-energy level.* The work can be very hard and can come at her from all directions, all at once. She must therefore possess an excitement and initiative that keeps her

going when it'd be much easier to back down and slack off. Reward this quality in her, especially after those particularly tough seasons when the work has been nonstop and she's given extra of her time. An afternoon off or some other way of saying thanks will help her maintain her passion for the work she does.

3. *Personal warmth and people skills.* Your assistant probably deals with more people in the course of a day than you do as the leader. And she represents you and your office to every single one of them. When people pick up the phone to call you, knowing that she will be the first to answer, you want them to expect a pleasant, inviting person on the other end—someone who makes them feel like they, too, are an important part of what you're all doing together.

4. *Integrity and trustworthiness.* She must be a person whose walk is consistent with her words, who possesses the highest character. You must be able to place your heart in her hands and know that it's safe there. The relationship between leader and assistant, like all others, rides on the rails of trust and honesty.

5. *Reliability.* Few things are more taxing to a leader's time and energy than having to constantly check to make sure his assistant has done what he asked. She needs to spend her time getting the job done, not looking for excuses. You're a blessed person if you, like I, have a capable, responsible assistant to whom you can give an assignment and forget it.

6. *Good self-image.* You want an administrative assistant who can handle herself with confidence, who feels good about herself and about life. She'll handle your office with the same demeanor.

7. *Mental horsepower and personal growth.* Your assistant's

knowledge and insight can be invaluable to you as a leader. She sees things and hears things that never come across your desk. She also provides you with a woman's perspective. It's often helpful to seek her discernment on how to handle an issue or decision. Seek an administrative assistant who desires to keep learning as the job expands, who thinks clearly and sees the details, who wants to be stretched and to grow in her position.

8. *Followship ability.* If your assistant loves you and the ministry, she'll find it easy to submit to your authority and to be a team player. You cannot have an assistant who bucks the system.

9. *Sense of humor.* Encourage her to find one thing to laugh about every day. Administrative assistants need to enjoy their job, the people they work with, and the congregation they serve. They need to mix some fun into their day. Even the serious work of leading and serving God's people has its lighter side. A good assistant will look for it, find it, and enjoy every minute of it.

10. *Flexibility.* It's hardly out of the ordinary for a pastor to be faced with an emergency, a matter requiring urgent, immediate attention. His assistant must be able to drop whatever she's working on at the time to help. She must not be totally knocked off guard by a sudden change in schedule or agenda. Flexibility also comes into play when dealing with new technologies, not being resistant to learning new skills and methods that can help her fulfill her calling to the greatest extent.

11. *Bounce-back skills.* Not every phone call or visitor she encounters each day is the kind that makes her glad she came to work in the morning. An administrative assistant

will get knocked down and run over at times. But the best know how to react to negative, discouraging situations by getting back to their feet and moving ahead as planned, bouncing back into their work with energy, a sweet attitude, and just the right amount of forgetfulness.

12. *Self-discipline.* Assistants simply cannot be procrastinators. Too many unknowns and unforeseens can crop up, and each one is more than capable of preventing the accomplishment of what she'd planned to do with her day. It's imperative that she strives to stay ahead of schedule, not putting things off. This will give her the space for reacting nimbly to unexpected situations while also helping her be more thorough with her many tasks, not always rushing to catch up from falling behind . . . again.

13. *Creativity and intuition.* Anyone can spot a problem. It takes an eager, imaginative person to spot a solution, to sense what's happening even without knowing all the facts. Assistants who can find creative ways to get things done on their own, rather than constantly asking for direction and guidance, will give you time to devote to other matters.

14. *The Big Picture thinking.* Assistants need to know your job just as well as their own. They need to be clear on what you're trying to accomplish, what your main objectives are. By seeing the tasks of the office through your eyes, she can more quickly and naturally understand what really needs doing. She can see beyond her own desk and find a larger purpose for being there.

15. *Absence of personal problems.* No one's life is problem free, but I'm sure you can name a few folks who are a constant soap opera. Far from dealing with the occasional

disruption or challenge, their lives are a never-ending cycle of chronic problems—problems that spill over onto everything (and everyone) they come into contact with. Your assistant needs to be someone who keeps her personal, family, and business life in order. Otherwise, your office will become a distracting clearinghouse for her revolving door of stories and complaints.

16. *Love for God.* The best quality anyone can bring to work with them in the morning is an essence of Christlikeness. If a person loves God and sees his or her life as a daily offering to His will and His way, they will relate with others as they should and will represent both the minister and the ministry appropriately. This is not an easy thing to quantify, but you know it when you see it.

17. *Loyalty.* Your assistant may not always agree with you, but she should always support you. When others make negative comments about you, your personality, or your decisions as a leader, your assistant should be the first to defend you. She should speak well of you, not falling in with those who are looking to find fault. Leaders are certainly capable of being wrong. We don't handle every situation perfectly or make the best calls in every circumstance. But there is a right place and time, just as there is a right way and method, for being held accountable for these matters. And being gossiped about behind your back is not one of them, especially by those who most directly assist you in ministry. You need to know that when your assistant talks about you in public, she's talking about your strengths and accomplishments, not your weak spots and downsides.

18. *Confidentiality.* Working in a minister's office naturally brings people, situations, and circumstances into light

that have no business being discussed in the church hall-
ways. Any breach of this private information, in my book,
is grounds for termination. Breaking confidence is a clear
disregard for the people your assistant is called to love and to
serve. The pastor's office is a junction point for all kinds of
serious problems and private concerns. People's lives are at
stake here, and they should not—*cannot!*—be treated flip-
pantly and with a flapping tongue.

19. *Love for the church.* The Father loves it, the Son died
for it, and the Spirit continues to nurture it. Your assistant,
therefore, must be a person who does everything she can
to love, support, and encourage the church's identity and
mission. Even if she attends another church besides yours,
she needs to be devoted to the calling that's been placed on
the congregation where she works throughout the week. A
church assistant who doesn't love the church is a contradic-
tion in terms.

20. *Representing you well.* One of the main blessings in
having an assistant who supports your God-given vision and
takes joy in your accomplishments is that it helps her be natural in representing you well to others. Even on the phone,
I love to hear Miss Ruth say to someone, "Pastor Johnny
would be pleased to meet with you," or "Pastor Johnny would
be honored to preach at your groundbreaking service." She
is a true extension of my ministry, a living extension of *me.*
Many people see me through the eyes of my assistant, and
they never fail to get a good impression. I cannot put a price
tag on that kind of asset.

21. *Being organized.* Ministry is so spontaneous, it's essential that we organize everything we possibly can. Otherwise,
we're out of whack all the time. And it doesn't take long for

people to notice it. You need your assistant to meet with you on Monday mornings to go over the weekly calendar and to set the basic outline and agenda for the week. Give her responsibility for organizing your schedule, your travels, your filing system, and all the details of the office. If you take too many of these jobs on yourself, you will have no time left for leading. Insist on an assistant who takes organization to a high level.

22. *Being detail-oriented.* The time saved by a leader whose assistant files things appropriately, spell-checks her correspondence, validates appointments, and even fills out telephone slips correctly cannot be adequately measured. In case she forgets or gets bogged down in such minutiae, remind her frequently of the high value you place on these efforts. Help her see that there's ministry happening with every staple, hole punch, and paper clip.

23. *Being a door closer.* Loose ends don't contribute anything but frustration to a leader's life. He needs to know that his assistant will finish the projects she's started under his direction and will do so on time and in a responsible fashion. Again, it's mighty distracting to have to look over her shoulder all the time, never really sure if her work is being done like you want and when you want it. Give her great affirmation for completing her tasks and for doing them well.

24. *Going above expectations.* When I hand my sermon to Miss Ruth each week to be typed, it always comes back to me looking crisp and clean, with little creative touches that make it even better. She improves on my performance. Encourage your assistant not to wall herself off behind her job description. When she goes the second mile, she takes the whole ministry with her.

25. *Sunshine.* It all starts and ends with the joy of Christ illuminating from her work and demeanor just as you hope it does from yours. Those who spread sunshine into other people's lives will never lack for friends or lunch companions. Look for an assistant who brightens the office space, reflecting the love of Jesus both in her excellent work and her enthusiastic outlook.

Your leadership is made all the better by those who support and encourage you. So put a great deal of time and thought into this key ministry relationship between you and your assistant. It's more than a job to fill; it's a calling to share. Try doing it without her, and you'll find out real quick that you're no match for the opposition.

Three Great Tests of Leadership

33

In school, you're taught a lesson and then given a test. In life, you're given a test that teaches you a lesson.

—TOM BODETT

B e sure of it. God will test you.

When Jesus asked His disciple Philip how they might be able to feed the thousands of people who were following them up a Galilean hillside, the Bible affirms that Jesus "asked this to test him" (John 6:6). Some who travel in Christian circles assume that anything challenging or uncomfortable in life must come from the devil, that a question like this would be something to rebuke, not receive. Many times, however, it is God Himself who is putting you in a situation to see how you'll handle it.

King David understood this . . . and invited it. He prayed, "Search me, God, and know my heart; test me and know my concerns. See if there is any offensive way in me" (Ps. 139:23–24). He didn't want the Lord to leave him like he was, unscrutinized and unproven. In order to grow, in order to lead, he needed to be tested. And he knew it.

But whether we know it or not, God will test us anyway— not to make our life miserable, not for the fun of seeing us squirm, but for the purpose of making us stronger, getting us ready, building our leadership muscle. The greatest of these tests tend to fall in the following three categories, each one (somewhat surprisingly) more difficult than the other:

1. *Adversity.* The Bible doesn't hold back from announcing this up front. Peter wrote, "Dear friends, when the fiery ordeal arises among you to test you, don't be surprised by it, as if something unusual were happening to you" (1 Pet. 4:12). This is normal. This is to be expected. Adversity is God's way of getting you up on your toes, prepared to fight and defend what matters most to you.

But how do you handle it, beyond just knowing it's coming? You handle it by letting adversity motivate you to throw your full weight on God, depending on Him for everything—the strength, the perseverance, the very will to continue. Rather than focusing on your enemy, on your pain, or on the issue itself, you put your complete trust in God to carry you through and to help you learn all the insight He desires for you to glean from the process.

In regard to any enemies who are coming against you, the Bible teaches you to turn the other cheek (Matt. 5:39), even to love and pray for them (Matt. 5:43–44), even to return good for the trouble they're causing you (Rom. 12:20–21). And in regard to the whole situation in general, we are taught to let God help us be glad about it:

"Blessed are you when they insult you and persecute you and falsely say every kind of evil against you because of Me. Be glad and rejoice, because your reward is great in heaven. For that is how they persecuted the prophets who were before you" (Matt. 5:11–12).

There's more than just having a good attitude, however, to handling adversity well. In recounting the times that King Saul was causing difficulty for David, God's Word commends David three separate times in 1 Samuel 18 for behaving wisely, for continuing to go faithfully about his business, not blinded by anger, revenge, or self-pity. When those in your church or organization are making things hard on you, it's still your job to maintain your focus and keep your relationships with them as intact and healthy as possible.

Oh, it's so natural to strike back at those who don't like you, those who are the quickest to criticize. If not lashing out, you at least feel like distancing yourself from them. But the truth is, these individuals are probably the ones who are most in need of your ministering hand and heart. So go ahead and invite conversations with them about sensitive subjects. Get things out in the open, not in hot debate but in honest discussion, initiating reconciliation on whatever matter is dividing you. Even if you don't get anywhere with them at first, you're at least building a bridge, a point of access that will keep the possibility for resolution open and available.

Keep these private battles private, just between the ones who are directly involved. Continue to practice kindness, which is often able to change hearts even when valid arguments cannot. The way you respond to others is as important—perhaps *more* important—than the words you say.

But remember this too: adversity almost always provides a mirror for you to see yourself more clearly, if you're brave enough for a peek. There is often some measure of truth to what's rankling a brother or sister about you. Look on this uncomfortable encounter as an opportunity both to be *re*proved as well as *im*proved. And pray that God will allow you to be *ap*proved, as well—shown to be right in your motivation and direction as the leader of your people. Adversity can accomplish all of this if you don't resist it out of hand.

2. *Prosperity*. Remember me saying that these tests get progressively harder? Then why does prosperity come next, after adversity? Don't take my word for it. Take it from Abraham Lincoln: "Nearly all men can stand adversity, but if you want to test a man's character, give him power." Give him stature. Give him authority. Give him prosperity.

Where adversity gets you *on* your toes, prosperity has an uncanny way of getting you *off* your toes. Adversity brings out the fighter in us, but prosperity brings out the sofa cushions and the hot fudge sundaes. It makes us fat, lazy, and satisfied. Soft, apathetic, and unalert. More than that, it can make us cocky and self-confident, forgetful of where we've come from and unsympathetic toward those who are still there. Prosperity is a pride inducer, a humility vacuum. And by causing us to lose our edge while gaining status, it can reasonably be said that prosperity claims more victims than even immorality.

I'm not saying to run from it; I'm saying to be very leery of it and to *never* put your trust in it.

Paul, of course, had the right approach when he said, "I know both how to have a little, and I know how to have a lot. In any and all circumstances I have learned the secret of being content—whether well-fed or hungry, whether in abundance or in need" (Phil. 4:12). When Paul possessed much, he knew how to use it and what not to conclude from it. Abundant grace—the constant recognition that the breath in our lungs and the hope in our heart is totally dependent on God alone—enabled him to bear abundant prosperity.

Most of us know how to be abased and do without; few have learned how to abound and do it well. The average man cannot steady the brimming cup of blessing without spilling some, without taking his own share of the credit and enriching himself with its bounty. Fullness *from* God often begets forgetfulness *of* God.

The Lord warned us through the prophet Amos, "Woe to those who are at ease in Zion" (Amos 6:1). If we ever start to think that comfort and luxury are the chief requirements of life, our days as a leader are numbered. Skim through a week of newspapers, and you'll notice the body count. Prosperity can kill dreams and visions just as thoroughly as outright adversity. Perhaps, in fact, it has done away with more. When advancement and achievement come, don't look at them as rewards. See them as tests. And be ready for a new breed of battle foes.

3. *Obscurity.* The deadliest of them all. Living and leading without recognition can take more from a man than any other enemy on earth. Perhaps nothing can test the motives of your heart and expose the true depth of your passion and calling more than being unknown, unrewarded, and unappreciated.

I often hear young pastors say that the church they're serving doesn't have much potential. Maybe that's true in some respects. But such a conclusion usually tells more about the person making the statement than about the place where he's working. What it often means is that "no one knows I'm out here." Therefore, the possibilities for building a résumé and reputation that can help him climb the pastoral ladder are hard to come by. Being off the main road can play tricks on a man's calling.

This is where a lot of people pack it in. This wasn't what they signed up for. This wasn't the image they had in their heads when God called them into pastoral ministry. The spiritual heroes who first inspired them weren't out here enduring a church that featured double-digit attendance on a good day. What difference can a man make with such meager pickings as these? What's the use when no one's here to listen?

I find it amazing that Jesus placed supreme emphasis on serving in obscurity. Three times in a matter of just a few verses, framed within some of the greatest teachings in all the New Testament, He took a hard stand against those whose primary motivation came from man-made applause (see Matt. 6:1–18). How easy it is to let their clapping become our drumbeat, their praise our main basis for perseverance. But Jesus had a rare gift in store for those who dared to keep giving, praying, and fasting even when no one was around to be impressed: "Your Father who sees in secret will reward you" (v. 4).

The platform is a nice place to stand, but rarely if ever a good place to start. Leaders—the ones who become great, the ones who know what they believe in, the ones who are built to survive storm and attack—are those who have honed their skills on the back side of nowhere, out where God was training them to serve for His glory and no one else's.

If that's where He's got you right now, be patient and persistent. Keep getting up and going. Don't look down on your surroundings or scorn the "day of small things" (Zech. 4:10). Realize that you render yourself the most unimpressive when you strive to impress others, but you serve God the best when recognition is not your real motivation. Let God do everything He's planned for you during this season of obscurity, so that you can become—like Paul—able to serve Him anywhere, under any condition or circumstance, always to the praise of His glorious, eternal, and all-powerful name.

Adversity will test your mettle, prosperity your momentum, and obscurity your motivation. Expect to meet all three along the way. And pray for what it takes to come forth proven and prepared. Thank God for caring enough about your success to test you in the process.

The Leader's Time Management

34

*Take care of the minutes, and the hours will
take care of themselves.*

—LORD CHESTERFIELD

You've got a thousand things to do—deadlines staring
at you, people depending on you, memos awaiting
your response, projects awaiting your attention. Your next
sermon still needs hours of preparation, but people need
your ministry, your staff needs your direction, and your
e-mails need an answer. And all of this stands on top of all
the other stuff you didn't finish last week . . . and the week
before that.

The leader's life can go around like this forever. Each
day can seem insurmountable, eaten up with random activity that keeps you busy but gets you nowhere. The highest

achievers, however, are those who master the practical techniques of time management and spin their schedules back in their favor. They've discovered that the key to managing their time is managing themselves, not micromanaging everyone and everything else.

Easy? No. But possible? Yes.

And like I said—very practical. Let's spend a few minutes getting extremely real about how to take back your calendar before it drives you any crazier. Here are thirteen things I've learned over the years that have given me my days back:

1. *Be time-conscious.* Ben Franklin said that time is "the stuff life is made of." Therefore, we must guard it at all costs. To fritter away our time is to fritter away our lives. So don't even *think* about ambling into your day without a plan and some clear priorities. You know as well as I do—it'll be gone before you know it. You'll spend all day reacting and never accomplishing your main objectives. Killing or losing time is a surefire way to bury your leadership potential.

2. *Get an early start.* Use the first part of your day to organize and prioritize. I get up nearly every morning around 5:45, taking advantage of these first moments of daylight to get my plans in order. I know that distractions will swarm and dive at me all day long, but in the quiet of the morning, distractions are at a minimum. So even while spending time in prayer and Bible reading, I keep my day-timer close, jotting down reminders as God brings them up. Here is where I realize again that our lives are not divided into the sacred and the secular. There should be as much worship and prayer involved in setting your schedule as in reading a devotional book. Ask God to bless and order your

day from its very outset, while also giving Him deliberate permission to upset your planned agenda if His will should override it.

3. *Show up on time.* The Proverbs capture the warning well: "How long will you stay in bed, you slacker? When will you get up from your sleep? A little sleep, a little slumber, a little folding of the arms to rest, and your poverty will come like a robber, your need, like a bandit" (Prov. 6:9–11). Proper time management begins with being at work on time . . . every day.

4. *Prioritize to W-I-N.* Make frequent use of this simple acrostic to keep you on task and on target. W-I-N: "What's Important Now?" Why would you want to be doing anything else?

5. *Think on paper.* Writing things down minimizes confusion and brings clarity and cohesion to your thoughts. That's why I often ask my staff to give me a written review on any proposal or project they're considering. If they can't articulate their ideas in print, chances are they haven't thought it through enough and don't yet understand what they're trying to accomplish. Getting it on paper helps to zero in on what really needs to happen and what kinds of questions still need answering.

6. *Stick with your system.* Whatever kind of time management method you decide to use, wear it out and make it work for you. Don't try interfacing two systems at once. Things are hard enough to keep your arms around without doing everything possible to streamline and simplify.

7. *Schedule your time in blocks.* Boy, this has really proven revolutionary for me. Rather than scattershooting various activities throughout your day, bunch similar tasks together

to avoid loss of concentration and wasted time traveling between venues. Here's how I do it: The early morning hours are my best time of day. So I routinely block these out for study. The only interruptions I'll tolerate during this stretch of time is an emergency or a family member who needs my attention. I generally schedule a block in the afternoon for returning all the day's phone calls, one after another, not all day long in the gaps between other things. I also bunch my appointments together as much as possible, such as meeting with my staff or having guests into my office. I might ask my assistant, for example, to schedule all my counseling sessions from 1:30 to 5:30 on a Tuesday afternoon rather than doing one in the morning, another later in the day, thus keeping me distracted and not able to bring my full self to each important meeting. You just want to avoid putting yourself into a position of having to constantly redirect your energies. You'll never get deep enough into any one project unless you put that time in its own little box, giving everything you can to one effort. Managing your time this way is not the same as being held hostage to a schedule. Rather, it's more like using your schedule as a compass, a way of keeping you moving forward without ever veering too far off course.

8. *Make good use of mealtimes.* Manley Beasley taught me this principle long ago, and I've benefitted from it ever since. I often schedule a breakfast, lunch, or dinner to meet with people who've asked to see me or to enjoy a time of deliberate fellowship. You're going to be eating anyway as a rule. Why not make it a double blessing and spend it with someone you've been needing to visit?

9. *Anticipate interruptions.* A schedule that doesn't leave room for the unexpected is an invitation for frustration. Real

life is way too good at disrupting things, and there's only so much you can do about it. Therefore, don't cram your calendar so full that it takes every spare minute to accomplish the weeks' priorities. Leave enough breathing room in there to accommodate interruption. I'll tell you what I've observed, though, which may be of help to you. I've noticed that most emergencies surface in the morning. By scheduling tasks through the mid-morning hours that are easier to come in and out of, you'll find yourself better able to respond to most of your sudden intrusions. I make a point, for example, of not scheduling any appointments before around 10:00 a.m. This keeps me reasonably free to handle the bulk of these problem interruptions.

10. *Beware the time eaters.* I know they mean well, but many of the people who ask if you've got a minute really mean *fifteen* minutes. And remember, "Got a minute?" is a question, not a demand. I'm not advocating rudeness here, but you must learn to be adept at discerning whether a person's request for your time is real ministry, work-related, or merely social. If it's social, that's often OK. But be ready at an appropriate time to say, "Well, my friend, I've enjoyed chatting with you. Have a nice day." Send a signal that you need to wrap this up and move on to other matters.

11. *Manage impromptu meetings.* Your feet are often your best ally in keeping off-the-cuff encounters from becoming long, drawn-out affairs. If someone catches you in the hallway, consider carrying on the conversation while you're walking to the place you were headed. If they stop by your office, stand to greet them and keep standing while you visit. Sitting down is an unspoken indicator that you're willing to engage in a long conversation. Save this for times when that's

really what you mean. Adrian Rogers taught me one of the best ways to handle a common occurrence: the person who comes up to you after the evening service and says, "Pastor, I need to drop by your office and see you this week. When would be a good time?" If they can wait for just a minute, ask them to sit down on a front pew and visit with you right then. In this way you'll be able to help that person with their particular concern while also saving yourself an extra meeting during the week, which invariably would have taken two to three times as long. Not every encounter, of course, is meant to be brief, but many of them can accomplish the same amount of business in half the amount of time. When you know you're in a situation where someone's threatening to want a big chunk of it, keep your comments to a minimum and get to the bottom line as quickly as you can.

12. *Don't feel attached to every e-mail.* Not everybody likes e-mail, but I do. I've found it to be a wonderful time-saving tool for many forms of communication. At the same time, it can cost you valuable hours each week if you're not careful with how you use it—especially with what it likes to demand of you. For example, I get a large number of e-mails that are forwarded to my in-box—little thoughts, news bits, and stories that people feel would be a blessing to me. But I've found that I don't have time to read my own e-mail and others' as well. There's no law that says you can't delete an unread, impersonal e-mail without thinking twice about it. I suggest that you make this your standard procedure.

13. *Wrap up the day.* Before leaving your office in the afternoon or evening, clear your desk, put everything back where it belongs, and enter the next day's to-do list on your calendar. This will reduce the stress of having to remember

something for the next day, plus you won't have to waste time clearing up the office first thing in the morning. Make the necessary preparations to start every day off as fresh as possible.

By gaining control of your time, you gain control of your life rather than giving it over to others who are more than happy to do it for you. After all, who better knows what you should be doing with your time than you do? And if you don't know, then you're not really leading.

Time is a gift. Unwrap it wisely.

The Leader and Mentoring

35

True heroism . . . is not the urge to surpass all at whatever cost,
but the urge to serve others at whatever cost.

—ARTHUR ASHE

We can talk and talk about leadership, but if we never take it beyond our own time zone—our own generation—we will spin our wheels till they won't spin anymore, and our influence will die *with* us instead of outlive us.

Leaders are called to be mentors.

Mentoring is sure to be one of the most fulfilling ministries you'll ever embark on. I shared in an earlier chapter on "Guiding Principles" how I've mentored a different young pastor each year (now *two* each year) through an intentional program at our church. I know of very few things in my life that bring me greater joy than knowing I am adding value to these young men's lives by attempting to model ministry to them. Seeing them grow and prosper and put down roots in their various places of service thrills my heart each time I hear from them or get a report on their progress. If you think leadership feels good when it's adding up to something, wait till you see how it feels when it's multiplying.

But if there's so much excitement and satisfaction to be found in mentoring, why are so few actually doing it? Why do we not rally in droves to the words of the apostle Paul, who said to his own protégé Timothy, "What you have heard from me in the presence of many witnesses, commit to faithful men who will be able to teach others also" (2 Tim. 2:2)?

Plain and simple, the answer is selfishness. It goes under a lot of other excuses that sound a little nicer and less condemning, but it's selfishness just the same, not to mention a shortsighted view of our time and talents, applying them only to the pressures of this moment without seeing them through the lens of eternity. Paul exhorted the Philippians to "do nothing out of rivalry or conceit, but in humility consider others as more important than yourselves. Everyone should look out not only for his own interests, but also for the interests of others" (Phil. 2:3–4). How many times have I mentioned in this book—and how true it is for all of us as leaders—that our work is all about *others?* Leading others. Caring for others. Investing in others. Believing in others. Mentoring is one of the most effective, long-lasting ways to live out this guiding principle. Ask yourself: What am I doing today that will guarantee my impact for Jesus Christ into the next generation? Mentoring is among the best of all possible answers.

But like everything of value, it takes time and commitment. You are building into the life of another person, not so much through a classroom lecture as through the example of your life and ministry heart. So expect it to require:

1. *Spiritual commitment.* Hopefully you're already well past playing games at the foot of the cross. You're dead serious about living a life that has major impact for Christ amid your circle of influence. Mentoring takes this kind of zeal and passion, an active desire to "get with it."

2. *Life change.* The day you stop growing is the day you stop ministering. That's why the best mentors are not the type who hand down their answers with a know-it-all pride and arrogance, but rather those who are always seeking to be more fruitful in service to their Lord. Having someone watching and learning from you as you do this will keep you encouraged to constantly improve.

3. *High moral values.* You will never be able to ultimately outrun the limitations of your own moral integrity. But by giving one or two others access to your life, you shut down one of Satan's favorite inroads to a leader's heart—the protection of spiritual disguise. To be an effective mentor, you must be who you claim to be. But good news: being a mentor will also *assist* you in being the person you really want to be.

4. *Clear objectives.* Mentoring should not just be a rambling walk in the park, a here-and-there experience with nothing to hold it together and no way to know when you've reached your intended purposes. Set measurable goals for what you and your followers need to accomplish during this time, and make a credible plan for getting there.

More daunting than the things mentoring requires, however, are the blessings it promises both to you and to the one (or ones) you're mentoring. Among its more exciting, enriching benefits are examples like these:

1. *It develops a person.* Mentoring gives you the rare treat of seeing someone grow by leaps and bounds before your very eyes. You get to relish their enthusiasm. You feel younger yourself by breathing in their eagerness. But nothing is quite as invigorating as knowing that you are helping someone to mature in Christ. Paul said that he was willing to "labor for this, striving with His strength that works powerfully in me" (Col. 1:29). I know how he feels, looking forward to heaven when we can see all that God did through us by letting us help a few individuals prepare for even greater things.

2. *It clarifies your priorities.* You learn a lot about yourself and what really matters in life when you try explaining it intentionally to others. If you have a hard time being very exact about what you hope to accomplish in life—what you truly feel you've been placed on earth by God to do— mentoring will help you eliminate some of the fluff and to concentrate on the meat.

3. *It builds leaders for tomorrow.* Again, there's only so much you can do in your lifetime, and only so many places you can be in a day. Investing yourself this deliberately into the life of another person expands your ministry into years you'll never get to see with human eyes. Live for now, but live also for the generations to come.

4. *It gives a sense of accomplishment.* Basically, mentoring just gives you a good feeling when you drive away from meeting with this person and when you lay down your head at night. You realize that you're multiplying your ministry. You realize that God has done more through your life than you ever really noticed before. You realize that He has

poured Himself into you with love, direction, opportunity, and challenge, and has done something special in you—one who could never claim to deserve the honor.

Yes, mentoring strengthens you personally—perhaps much more than it does for the one you're mentoring. It gives you deep relationship with young men who are set to carry the mantle of ministry with real passion and creativity. These people become eternally precious to you, just as Paul declared: "For who is our hope, or joy, or crown of boasting in the presence of our Lord Jesus at His coming? Is it not you? For you are our glory and joy!" (1 Thess. 2:19–20).

Pray that God would direct someone into your life, someone to whom you can pass along the blessings and lessons the Lord has entrusted to you. Begin to look for them—men who are hungry, men who are teachable. And ask God to give you a specific plan for carrying out the ministry of mentoring. You'll find that you have more to say and share than you probably thought at first.

I'm grateful to God for the day in Tianjin, China, when He spoke into my life and made it clear to me that for the rest of my years of pastoring, I should be mentoring young men. I thank Him for the privilege of having a Timothy+ Barnabas school where hundreds of pastors have come from all over America—and even from several countries around the world—to share times of encouragement and instruction. Mentoring has become something I don't know how to live without anymore. I'm absolutely convinced you'll feel the same way.

Leaders Making a Difference

36

The only ones among you who will be really happy are those who have sought and found how to serve.

—ALBERT SCHWEITZER

Today may just look like any other day. Another page to turn in your calendar. Another coffee and a bagel. Another drive to the office. Just like yesterday.

But it's ordinary days like these that comprise a life. And if our hearts aren't serious about making a difference this morning, this afternoon, this evening before we go to bed, we'll wake up one ordinary day and wish we had another. We'll wish we'd done more when we had the chance. We'll wish we hadn't viewed our meetings, appointments, and planning sessions as ordeals to slog through but as opportunities to effect lasting change.

Leaders don't make a difference by rallying people's enthusiasm at some big event or by launching major programs and initiatives. They make a difference by going full throttle on the Tuesday nights and Thursday mornings when everyone else is watching TV or reading cereal boxes. They make a difference by being *everyday* difference makers. That's what I've always wanted to be.

Each time the Lord has led me to begin pastoring a church, I've never seen it as a position to fill but as a challenge to embrace. If I was going to be serving there, I might as well be leading these people to make a dent in the kingdom of darkness and make a difference for the kingdom of God. I can sit here today and tell you that this passion has never dried up or grown the least bit stale for me. On the contrary, it burns more white-hot in me this very hour than it did this time a year ago. Making a difference. Changing the landscape. Going all out. We don't do anybody any favors by settling for less.

If I had to put my finger on the three things that are most important when striving to lead for maximum change, I'd name these:

1. *Be intentional.* Today starts with a purpose in mind. Do you know what yours is? If you don't, you certainly can't expect to make any progress toward fulfilling it. Begin thinking more intentionally about everything you do, not wasting the daily experiences and encounters that are bulging with possibility for those who see them that way. When I stand to preach and proclaim the Word of God, I have a particular purpose in mind about what I'm saying. And if I'm going to be a leader and life changer, I need to have the same kind of intention when I go to the bank window,

or take a walk through my neighborhood, or sit down at a staff meeting. What am I needing to accomplish here? Who would the Lord lead me to speak with today? What is God's will for this next two hours in my afternoon? This may sound mighty radical to those who like to lollygag through life, not overthinking things or getting too bent out of shape. But you're a leader. You're a difference maker. And nobody does much of either if they're not intentional about it.

2. *Be relational.* I'm not sure there's a stronger, more significant word in the leader's vocabulary. We're not out to change structures and programs and processes but *people*— people who need God, who need encouragement, who need guidance, who need tools for life and the motivation to use them. Our visions and goals and dreams should not just be diagrams on a restaurant napkin. They are transformations in people's whole lives and outlooks. And in order to see them through to this end, we must be serious—intentional— about engaging ourselves in significant ways with others on a regular basis. Every time you meet with a person, be thinking about how you can add value to his or her life. Be thinking about how you could help the person experience more of God's victory through Christ. Be thinking about what God would have you to say—or perhaps what God would have you to *hear* as you listen to him or her. The only differences worth making are those that are made in others' lives. You earn the right to make them when you take the time to seek relationship.

3. *Be practical.* It may seem merely spiritual to some that Jesus came and died and rose again, that He enters any human heart who becomes desperate for His grace and accepts Him by faith. To me, though, the results of this

glorious transaction are also very practical. If the God who is drawing the world to Himself is the same God who lives and operates in me, it just stands to reason that my job as a leader—my job as a Christian, our job as a church—is to draw others to Him as well. This is as practical a mandate as it is a spiritual one. It means thinking specifically about what others need and how to show them, to tell them, to demonstrate for them that Jesus meets this need in the most complete way possible. It means encouraging our people not to view evangelism as a clinical exercise but as a natural, living part of their day, whether it's chatting with the refrigerator repairman or extending a kindness to the guy who swipes your membership card at the gym. Leadership, like all of life—even Christian life—is much more practical than we give it credit for. By seeking to be practical in your teaching and methods, you will avoid talking over people's heads and will make a real difference in people's hearts.

Sometime soon, lay all of your leadership activities and attitudes out on the table and see what they could become if these three words really got into them. How could they be more intentional, more relational, more practical? The conclusions you come to could make a world of difference.

Leaving It Different Than You Found It   37

We all leave footprints in the sand; the question is,
will we be a big heel, or a great soul.

—ANONYMOUS

As I stated in the previous chapter, the path that leads to making a difference is not as mystical as it is practical. Sound principles and common sense go a lot further than we sometimes realize in making incredible inroads for Christian transformation in the lives of our people.

This is especially true in those situations where you're facing stubborn resistance to your efforts at advancing the kingdom and bringing about change. The way you navigate these choppy waters requires much prayer and time with the Lord, to be sure, but also some very shrewd means of handling the strained dynamics of real-world leadership.

With this supposition in mind, I offer you five highly practical tips for moving your church, group, or organization to the next level of unity and effectiveness. These are the kind of everyday undertakings that can help you consistently overachieve, moving your vision forward even when certain forces are working hard to hold you back. Do it long enough and well enough, and you'll leave a mark on this world that will never rub off—and surprise a lot of people who never thought you could do it:

1. *Move with the movers.* I remember Mark Corts, then an adjunct professor at Southeastern Baptist Theological Seminary, teaching this simple principle to us when I was a young student there. I've never forgotten it, and it's proven itself true time and again in my leadership experience. Not everyone, you well know, will buy in to the direction and program God has given you to implement. There are doubters, do-nothings, and naysayers in every organization. I'm not saying that there might not be validity to some people's complaints. Nor am I saying that we should villainize any resistance to our ideas and treat their spokesmen as being unspiritual and subversive. But you can waste a lot of time and misdirect a lot of energy trying to convince certain people of things they will never accept, no matter how sound your reasoning or how certain you are of God's leading. Yet there always seems to be a core group in any fellowship that just wants what Jesus wants, that is always on board for whatever will make the most impact for good and the gospel. *Find that group!* Discern those who show every sign of walking intimately with their Lord and Master. Rather than trying to get every single person's approval, run with those whose obvious

motivation is *God's* approval. Lead from your strengths. And move with the movers.

2. *Lead positively.* If you ever descend to being combative and negative, you've lost your platform for leadership. Opposition will come. People will frustrate you. Some will act as though their calling in life is to block you at every turn and discredit everything you're trying to accomplish. But rather than obsessing over those who are working against you, continue to affirm those who are joining you in your dream and vision. Allow them ways to give testimony to what God is doing in their lives and in your church. In fact, when you've said everything you know to say and have *still* failed to convince those who are aligned against you, other people in your fellowship may be your best way to influence opinion. Stay upbeat and positive. It will serve you well over time.

3. *Don't respond publicly to negative sentiment.* This is another aspect or flip side of the previous point that's worth mentioning specifically. Don't use your pulpit as a weapon. If you decide to take up a personal vendetta in a public way, you run the risk of alienating additional people and destroying whatever chance you have at reconciliation with those who are already resisting your leadership. Besides, most of the people in your audience won't have a clue what you're talking about. And if one of the prime goals of your leadership is unity in your congregation—as it should be—you'll become an agent against it by injecting confusion and new waves of contempt into the corporate conversation. This is no way to deal with a problem person. Instead, love them. Affirm them. Pray for them. Serve them. Even though you know who they are and what they're trying to do, make it

your goal to help them discover God's best for their lives. They may turn on *you*, but don't you turn on *them*.

4. *Lead by example.* Be what you are challenging your people to become. Spend as much or more time *emulating* your message as you do *exhorting* them through your message. People follow what they see a whole lot more readily than what they hear. You may be serving a group of people who are a long way from exemplifying the kingdom-minded traits you know they need if the "gates of hell" are to have any reason for being worried in your city or community (see Matt. 16:18). But rather than doing a lot of harping and cajoling, the best way to inspire people to grow is to be growing yourself. Let them see in you what you're wanting to see in them. I talk to many young pastors who say, "I would never go to that church because they don't have this and this and this and this," to which I often say, "Maybe that's why they need *you*." Get out there and lead by example.

5. *Remind them of the vision consistently.* We've talked plenty in this book about the importance of casting a clear, credible vision before your people. But it's not enough to draw it up on paper and mention it once or twice from the pulpit. This gives the impression—or perhaps exposes the reality— that your vision is not nearly as connected to the everyday workings of the church as it should be. Make the vision a part of everything you do. Keep it right there in the driver's seat with you, like a compass that guides your various turns and decisions. Don't just *have* a vision; *use* your vision to steer all your activities and outreaches toward a consistent end. Communicate it often so that everyone knows about it, from the children and teenagers to the deacons and committee chairmen. When everyone feels a part of the team and knows

what the main objectives are, you can do a lot better job of coaching them.

It's hard enough to make a difference in life simply because the world is so full of ways to defeat and deflate you. It's doubly hard when some of the worst deflators come to live inside the walls of your church with you, stifling your progress and questioning your reasons for even being here. This doesn't get to be the end of the story, however—not for those leaders who aren't about to let a little opposition spoil God's overall purposes for your people. It may take a bit of creativity, a dash of self-discipline, and a whole lot of courage; but you can leave your place of service much better than you found it, even if some wish you'd just leave and go someplace else.

The Leader
as a Pioneer

38

We the youthful sinewy races, all the rest on us depend,
Pioneers! O pioneers!

—WALT WHITMAN

You certainly weren't drawn to leadership by a desire to
stack papers in neat piles or fill orders with the push
of a button. You were drawn instead by a desire to create
and initiate, to step to the front, leading the way onto paths
that are low on maps and procedure manuals but high on
potential and possibility.

The Lord Jesus was this kind of leader. When the writer
of Hebrews referred to Him as the "author and finisher of
our faith" (12:2 NKJV), the word *author* carries the con-
notation of a pioneer. Only a pioneer trailblazer would
accept the unprecedented challenge of living a perfect life,

laying down His life for helpless and rebellious sinners, then taking it up again to promise them victory over even the mortal enemies of death and the grave. Like a foot soldier clearing the path for the main body of troops, He advanced ahead of us in the spirit of the pioneer, going where none of us could go so that we could follow in the path He had cleared for us.

O pioneers!

We need you desperately. Most of the territories ahead are unknown and uncharted. That's why people fear them. They have no desire to enter dangerous areas that hold the threat of risk and loss. They don't think it necessary to bite off this kind of task. The thought of it makes them want to run home and throw the bedcovers over their heads.

But God has given you the heart of a leader, the grit of a foot soldier, the zeal and bravery of a pioneer. And though this doesn't mean you never feel afraid or unsure of yourself, it does mean that giving in to fear is not an option. Too many people are depending on you. They can't see what you see, can't deal with the cost involved, can't discern how desperate the need. It's going to take a leader—a pioneer—to march out ahead of the army and point the way to forward progress. God has gifted you for the challenge and has called you for this moment. He's been preparing you, through testing and trail, for all that lies ahead. This is where your leadership will jump off the business card and jump into the battle.

That's why you feel consumed by the dream you envision for the future. That's why you rise up from prayer with a sure word from the Lord, eager to grasp His invisible hand and pursue what He has told you to believe. That's why you wake up with a fire in your belly that refuses to be quenched by 9:00 a.m. coffee breaks and the shackles of standard procedure. You are exploring unclaimed land, wading into uncharted water, and anxious for your followers to see what it looks like out here—out in new vistas where your church, group, or organization has never ventured before.

Lead them there. Be the pioneer.

When Jesus was agonizing in the garden in preparation for His betrayal and death, the Scripture says that "going a little farther, He fell facedown and prayed" (Matt. 26:39). "Again, a second time, He went away and prayed. . . . After leaving them, He went away again and prayed a third time" (vv. 42, 44). He was blazing a trail that His followers could not yet see. No one can now deny that what He saw and what He was set to accomplish was worth whatever risk the challenge called for. He saw the salvation of sinners in His eyes. He saw the fulfillment of His Father's will. He saw glory and victory and the gift of eternal hope for generation after generation of hopeless humanity. So He kept going. A little further . . . a little further. Once, twice, again a third time, and on until the work was accomplished. A pioneering trailblazer is one who continues moving forward, leading the way to lasting change.

And as you go, be sure the following four essentials are zipped into your pack:

1. *Great vision.* It's been said that if you don't see it *before* you see it, you'll *never* see it. The Bible speaks of Moses persevering "as one who sees Him who is invisible" (Heb. 11:27). He was a man not only of insight but also of foresight. He could see down the road. He could look past the many good excuses for staying behind and see the far

horizons beckoning, calling him beyond the safe and the expected. As you pray, as you meditate on the Word, as you read, as you visit with others, ask God for a far-reaching vision. Difficulties will no doubt come, in all flavors and varieties, in all shapes and sizes. You'll never lack for them, so don't sit around waiting till they go away before choosing to advance. Focus instead on a place beyond your problems and ministry borders. Cast your gaze to the end rather than toward the reasons for not beginning. As George Bernard Shaw said, "Some men see things as they are and ask, 'why?' I dream things that never were and say, 'why not?'"

2. *An unencumbered spirit.* In what I'm about to say, please do not hear me advocating that you should never listen to others or receive any criticism as though it has merit. Neither you nor I know everything, and we can get our spiritual signals crossed just as easily as anyone. But pioneers are called to color outside the lines and to resist restrictions. People will do their best to fence you in and bottle up your potential. They'll feel uncomfortable with where a spirit like yours can lead. But a pioneer can't survive in a system that continually ties him down. You are more passion-driven than procedure-driven. You would rather die with your boots on under a wide-open sky than live under the artificial heat and light of a standard-issue office building. Certainly there is value in order and measure and gifted people who provide these necessary functions. But your role as a leader is not to sit inside and count time. It's to go out and change things.

3. A *daring heart.* Only the person who risks is really free—free to be actively involved in the mysterious workings of God's kingdom on earth, the only pursuit that's really

worth embracing. Paul was certainly a man of daring and risk taking. He said, "My aim is to evangelize where Christ has not been named, in order that I will not be building on someone else's foundation" (Rom. 15:20). Why keep churning up the same ground as everyone else, doing the same things that others are already doing, when God has given you a dream and vision as unique as your own leadership calling? The hiker walks a path already beaten down and civilized. It's the trailblazing pioneer who cuts through the tangled vines of opposition to clear a path that others can follow. If you fear that a lack of daring willingness has kept you locked inside the box, missing out on the excitement of God's best for your life, endeavor to ask, "Why not?" See what might be waiting on the other side.

4. *Deep faith.* True and lasting faith, of course, begins with faith in God. He alone is the power, the person, the presence—everything that's needed to move through uncharted waters. But pioneers also have faith in themselves, faith in what God can do through them when they remove all limitations to being used in His service. God says to you, "Look, I am the Lord, the God of all flesh. Is anything too difficult for Me?" (Jer. 32:27). He is the One who has placed this dream in your heart. So put your faith in Him—all of it—trusting completely in His ability to make you a pioneer. Trust, too, in your people, in those who lead underneath you as well as those who follow. Believe that the sovereign God—the giver of your vision—has also seen to it that you are surrounded by the people who can best join you in making an eternal difference.

Leadership is definitely not for the faint of heart. It's for those who—like you—have much more in mind than clinging to handrails and tiptoeing across stepping-stones. The place you're leading your followers may not be set in concrete and lined with running lights. But because God is in it—and because He has called you to it—future success is closer than it may seem at first sight. Be bold. Be brave. Be a trailblazer. Light the path, and those who long to live for God will follow.

Leaders Living with Risk

39

To conquer without risk is to triumph without glory.

—Pierre Corneille

The previous chapter was primarily taken up with what a pioneer must become in order to be effective as a leader. Before we leave the subject, however, it's only fair to be honest about what a pioneer must also *over*come.

This is the kind of thinking that differentiates between trailblazing and recklessness. Although pioneers are indeed called to be big and bold in their action, they are foolish to interpret this as meaning they should just take off without checking the oil, the gas tank, and the tire pressure. Many risks and legitimate concerns should be taken into account—not to slam the door on what God has led you to do but to help you follow Him with wisdom and understanding.

To do otherwise is careless and out of reality. For although sheer courage is to be admired, there's still a lot to be said for common sense in the mind-set of a leader.

Among the risks to be expected are these:

1. *The risk of rejection.* As a pioneer leader, you definitely need to introduce some thick-skinned-building exercises into your overall workout routine. Because heaven knows you're going to need it. Grumblers and gossips will nip around the edges, while the outright and outspoken will voice their disapproval to your face. Rejection will come. If it doesn't, in fact, you're probably not being bold enough in your leadership. The Bible teaches, however, that "the fear of man is a snare, but the one who trusts in the Lord is protected" (Prov. 29:25). Rejection doesn't have to get the last word. Persevere in your pioneering, and you will win over many of your detractors as God performs His unmistakable work in your midst.

2. *The risk of ejection.* One thing can be said of Job's friends: though they were downright depressing to have around, at least they were there. Who knows how many others of his friends didn't even bother to show up. As you begin leading with trailblazing vision, many of those who start with you will not hang around to finish with you. They're like the people who responded to Elisha's vision of God's plenty by saying, "Look, even if the Lord were to make windows in heaven, could this really happen?" The prophet answered their lack of faith with these words: "You will in fact see it with your own eyes, but you won't eat any of it" (2 Kings 7:2). Many will look back over their shoulders to see that God has used you to accomplish great things for the kingdom, but they will miss the joy of tasting and seeing

"that the Lord is good" (Ps. 34:8). You must continue on, even as others—even those close to you—choose to drop off along the wayside.

3. *The risk of dejection.* Some of the toughest battles faced by the pioneer leader happen inside his own headgear. All this quibbling and quitting—the rejection and ejection—can get inside your heart if you're not careful, leaving you too discouraged to keep going. But when a leader decides that the cost of ministry is too high, when he determines that he doesn't have what it takes to press on toward the fulfillment of his dreams, he's just then established the ceiling for his ministry. One thing we know about God is that He doesn't think in terms of ceilings and limitations. Therefore, through keeping your relationship with Him open and honest, staying continually refreshed by His Spirit, you must reject the first sign of dejection in your heart. It'll put your pioneering passion out to pasture.

Add to these the risk of failure, the risk of not staying faithful for the long haul, the risk of fatigue and weariness that can sling across your shoulders like dead weight, making even the feeblest efforts require more energy than you have on hand. But pioneers have their scopes out for these kinds of enemies lurking on the path. Their protective weapons are ready, quick to keep the path clear of roadblocks that serve no other purpose but to derail the mission.

Risk. No one ever led people toward great accomplishment without facing it by the boatload. The difficulty and demands of the task will scare many away, making the second-mile walk feel mighty lonely indeed. But the pioneer follows the words of Abraham Lincoln, "I do the best I know, the very best I can, and I mean to keep on doing it to the end. If the end brings me out all right, what is said against me will not amount to anything. If the end brings me out all wrong, ten angels swearing I was right would make no difference."

Don't go in unprepared. But do go undeterred.

Traits of a
Great Leader

40

Leaders must be close enough to relate to others,
but far enough ahead to motivate them.

—JOHN MAXWELL

W e've looked at so many topics and issues together. I'm delighted that you've chosen to follow along with me, hopefully adding to your leadership résumé with each turn of the page. I want to close by summing up a few of the main ideas I've observed over many years as a leader and pastor, thoughts I have included in various corners and chapters of this book. The following is a one-chapter summary of the essentials—my best attempt at answering the big question, "What makes a great leader?"

One word of caution, though, before we finish. It's quite easy for us to excuse ourselves from being great. We don't typically view our own contributions as being all that special. Knowing ourselves as well as we do, it's hard for us to imagine God going out of His way to raise up fruitful ministries around us. The challenge of even coming close to exemplifying the many qualities of great leaders, what with the scores of demands on our time and energy—well, what can anyone really expect of somebody like us?

But oh, my friend, God has called you to greatness—to make a difference where you are. To get the most from what He's given you. To open your heart for His full equipping, never settling for less than the complete accomplishment of His purposes for your life and leadership.

So make the following list your prayer list. Turn these ideals into measurable goals you can pursue with passionate abandon. Plug your ears to everything that doubt and discouragement have to say, and open your heart to everything God wants to do through your life in the months and years to come.

Your résumé hasn't fully been written yet. There's still a spot for greatness, waiting right beside your name, inscribed on the back are greatness traits like:

1. *Truthfulness and honesty.* If honesty is not 100 percent present in your leadership, you have no real right to relate to your people. Think of it: the reason you have a relationship with God at all is because He is totally honest and truthful. Were He not, how would you know from one day to the next that you were secure in His love and grace, that His Word could be trusted in every situation? Hasn't He proven truthful, even at the greatest possible cost to Himself? No matter what may frighten you away from being totally out front and above board with your people, nothing is more

dangerous than living behind a lie—even a relatively small one. As the Bible says, "A false witness will not go unpunished, and one who utters lies will not escape" (Prov. 19:5). You can easily be tempted to skew statistics, to misrepresent points of view, to hold back information in order to get your way in a committee meeting. But it will cost you your leadership if even the slightest hint of dishonesty hovers around you. "Lying lips are an abomination to the Lord, but those who deal truthfully are His delight" (Prov. 12:22 NKJV).

2. *Integrity.* As I've said, integrity speaks of wholeness in every area of life, a level of character and morality that pervades both your public and private demeanor. It's not a call to utter perfection—no one can achieve that, of course—but integrity does mean that others should be able to surprise us in any situation or setting and still find us acting honorably. This is particularly true in dealing with money and sexual morality—with gold and girls, with finances and females. These have historically been the key sites of character breaks that have brought down mighty men of God, tumbling their leadership into ruin and disgrace. The Lord said of Job, speaking to the devil, "He still retains his integrity, even though you incited Me against him" (Job 2:3). May the same be said of each of us.

3. *Passion.* This will always be high on my list of imperatives for leadership. People are attracted to passionate leaders, willing to follow them and take up places of service. But be prepared for some to be repelled by your passion. Do not let this deter you, however, from holding strongly to the convictions you cherish and the calling God has given you. Leadership is not something to be dabbled in, tried on, or toyed with. Leadership is something you must be consumed

by. When you have decided what must be done, immerse yourself in it. Stay passionate, or get out and let someone else drive.

4. *Caring and compassion*. These traits may already be in your nature, but in order to exemplify them as a leader and to keep from losing them along the way, caring and compassion must also be on your calendar. It's with good reason that caring is often spelled T-I-M-E. Though a thousand things interfere, making even the smallest acts of compassion inconvenient, they are rarely forgotten. They communicate your appreciation and value for others, and they keep you connected to what really matters in life. Dale Carnegie said, "You can make more friends in two months by becoming interested in other people than you can in two years of trying to get people interested in you." It'll cost you precious time to be caring toward others, but it will be among the most precious time you ever spend as a leader.

5. *Graciousness*. Think of it in contrast to its opposite: harshness. The Bible describes God as being "compassionate and gracious . . . slow to anger and abundant in faithful love" (Ps. 86:15). So how can we as leaders—and also as His servants—ever feel justified in being irritable and overbearing with those who look to us for direction? Graciousness is God's grace turned inside out. It's the Golden Rule in action. It's leadership at its most basic level of behavior.

6. *Gratitude*. An ungrateful heart is a sure indication that you don't understand life very well. If you did, you'd know that your calling and position are gifts from God's hand, privileges based on nothing else but His good pleasure, not on anything you've done without Him. If that's your posture—as it should be—then gratitude will grow

quite naturally on you. You'll be routinely aware that you are the result of contributions made by many people in your life, as well as people who came behind you—before you were ever in the picture—to build the foundation of your church or business. Gratitude in a leader helps you keep a bigger view, less focused on yourself, less consumed by pride in your own accomplishments. It keeps you living in reality, able to be more attuned to the needs around you and the many people who make your leadership go.

7. *Generosity.* Legacies are made by giving, not by acquiring. As Calvin Coolidge said, "No person was ever honored for what he received. Honor has been the reward for what he gave." You don't have to be a man of great wealth to be known as a giving person and leader. The only requirement is a willing spirit, the kind that not only gives on a whim but also *plans* to be generous with his time, money, talents, and resources. Perhaps nothing speaks more loudly or serves you better as a leader than maintaining a generous spirit. Be a person who finds his greatest joy in giving and sharing.

8. *Forgiveness.* Interact with enough people as a leader, and it won't be long before someone does something to offend or aggravate you. But you can't continue to be an effective influence in their lives unless you determine to quickly forgive, resisting every temptation to hold a grudge. Leaders—especially Christian leaders—are called to bless their followers, not to bless them out. Our example of this is the Lord Jesus. The Bible instructs us to "be kind and compassionate to one another, forgiving one another, just as God also forgave you in Christ" (Eph. 4:32). Was He willing to let us remain at a distance from Him because of our sins? Can you imagine Jesus saying, "OK, I forgive you, but

I don't want anything to do with you." Leadership is built on relationships, and relationships are restored and kept alive through the ongoing gift of forgiveness. People will not rally around bitterness and negativity.

9. *Encouragement.* I love what this word says because it's so descriptive of what people need, and such a great reminder of the privilege we bear as leaders. To encourage other persons is, by definition, to infuse "courage" into their hearts. It's just the opposite of what happens when we *dis*courage others, yanking the spirit and bravery right out of them. Encouragement fans the flickers and sparks of people's potential into the flame of ongoing achievement. So while a pat on the back may be only a few vertebrae north of a kick in the pants, it's miles ahead in terms of results. Seek every opportunity to encourage others.

10. *Friendliness.* It doesn't take much more than a fourth-grade understanding to realize that the one qualification for acquiring friends is to be a friend. The Bible states the obvious by reminding us, "A man who has friends must himself be friendly" (Prov. 18:24 NKJV). But sometimes—for some reason—this grammar school assumption can be lost on grown men. Not, however, on those who aspire to be great leaders, who know that friendliness makes people feel like they belong, endearing them to you and to your vision. It's still true that "a friend loves at all times" (Prov. 17:17), not getting in another's way unless he or she happens to be going down. Those who lead well are those who embody true friendship, not with an eye toward manipulating and making others beholden to you, but rather to be a blessing in others' lives.

11. *Influence.* The greatest way to know success is to

help others succeed. If God has blessed you with a measure of influence—and He has—use that influence to impact others for God and for good. Don't be afraid to exercise it. This will often mean standing on platforms and convictions that are unpopular, situations that open you up to ridicule and misunderstanding. But continue to hold to the truths you know from Scripture and from long experience to be solid and genuine. Refuse to let your influence be diluted by compromise or destroyed by sinful weakness. As pastor and writer Shelton Smith has said, "A man who has strong conviction but who is weak on courage is only slightly ahead of the man who has no convictions at all." Be a faithful steward of the influence God has given. Recognize its precious value. And use it for those things He initiates within you as you walk with Him by faith.

12. *Leadership.* This may sound redundant and unnecessary, but it bears being stated that leaders need to be leaders, not pointers. Many people think they are leading when they're not totally invested in the cause they're championing. But it can never be this way for great leaders. Jesus didn't merely *point* the way to taking up one's cross daily and following Him; He *led* the way by taking up His cross and being nailed to it. As I've said throughout the book, leadership is not a position to gain but a mission to embrace, a cause for which you're willing to sacrifice. Don't be all talk and little action. Don't be all action but little progress. Be a leader who lives and loves his leadership role enough to die for it.

You'll never go wrong as a leader if you hold yourself to these twelve attributes. You'll be the kind of person who is strong enough to lead but also strong enough to serve. And by mixing godliness with a God-given vision—and communicating it with clarity and energy—others will be drawn to what the Lord has started in you.

I'm proud to be counted among your number. And I'm praying for your continued success. ▣

Lord, how I thank You for this person who so desires Your will and way, whom You have bestowed with obvious gifts of leadership from Your gracious hand and who longs to use them for Your honor and glory.

May You equip him with everything required to fulfill Your calling in his life. May You surround him with others—people who are similarly called of God to their various ministries and responsibilities—who together with him can show the world what happens when You are at work in united, surrendered hearts.

May You keep him, Lord, close and clean. May his time with You each day be filled with worship and new understanding from Your boundless supply of wisdom. May his communication with You be both honest and earnest. Reward his deep desire to know You by hearing his prayer and showering forth Your faithful provision in his life.

Cement his calling, Lord God, if there is any lingering doubt in his heart. Bolster his confidence if there is any fear. Stir his passion if life and circumstances have conspired to dim his zeal. Renew. Rekindle. Remake what has been misused or mishandled.

*And inside his redeemed heart, may You steadily
increase in stature as he cedes ever-new territory
to Your complete control, letting You be the One who
leads through him, transforming lives,
communities, and even the current culture by
Your power and grace.*

*This is Your man, and You are his God. Why should
he fear or be discouraged? Settle him in what You have
planned for his life before the foundation of the world.
And may Your name be forever praised through
his leadership and legacy.*

In Jesus' name,

Amen.